REALSIMPLE

dinner tonight: done!

189 quick and delicious recipes

recipes edited by Allie Lewis Clapp and Lygeia Grace

REALSIMPLE   Time
HOME ENTERTAINMENT

It's 5 P.M.—do you know where tonight's dinner is? Why is that such a hard question to answer? Because, in no particular order: You're busy; you have a family; you have a job; you have a hobby; you're reading a great book; you're watching pets do funny things on YouTube; you're cleaning the bathroom; you're catching up with an old friend; you're planning your next vacation; you *(gasp!)* hate to cook. Or you simply have better things to do than spend all afternoon planning and preparing a meal that will take all of 15 minutes to consume.

Besides, Allie Lewis Clapp has the answer for you. As *Real Simple*'s food director, she, along with her talented team, is the genius responsible for the recipes in this book and therefore for your happiness tonight and tomorrow night and for many nights to come. These 189 recipes literally run the gamut from soups (pages 20 to 43) to nuts (page 321). Whether you want to build your dinner around meat or vegetables, in just half an hour or in only one pot, here you'll find delicious, healthy, easy dinners that will allow you to watch YouTube, read a book, or work really hard all afternoon and still have a satisfying meal in front of you by sundown. And, if you're up to it, a nice little dessert to finish.

But wait, you say, what if the cupboard is bare? No worries: We've got you covered. You may not be able to make our Thai Red Curry Chicken (not everyone has red curry paste in her pantry), but chances are you've got onions, cheese, beef broth, and bread—in which case you could make French Onion Soup without a trip to the market. The recipes use only real, whole ingredients, span cultures (from Moroccan Chicken Salad to Cuban Braised Beef), and are accompanied by helpful tips, tricks, and substitutions. You'll also find the nutritional breakdowns for all the recipes (page 346) and handy charts with pan substitutions, temperature conversions, and more (page 344).

It's 5 P.M.—do you know where tonight's dinner is? Of course you do. It's right here. Find it, make it, and enjoy.

Kristin van Ogtrop

Kristin van Ogtrop
Managing Editor, *Real Simple*

dinner tonight:
appetizers

spiced beef empanadas with lime sour cream

hands-on time: 35 minutes / total time: 1 hour
serves 8

1 tablespoon olive oil
1 small onion, chopped
½ pound ground beef
⅓ cup golden raisins
2 tablespoons ketchup
¼ teaspoon ground cinnamon
  Kosher salt and black pepper
2 refrigerated rolled piecrusts
1 large egg, beaten
½ cup sour cream
¼ teaspoon lime zest

▶ Heat oven to 375° F. Heat the oil in a large skillet over medium heat. Add the onion and cook, stirring occasionally, until soft, 5 to 6 minutes.

▶ Add the beef to the skillet and cook, breaking it up with a spoon, until no longer pink, 3 to 4 minutes. Stir in the raisins, ketchup, cinnamon, ½ teaspoon salt, and ¼ teaspoon pepper. Remove from heat.

▶ Using a 2½-inch round cookie cutter, cut out 24 circles from the piecrusts. Divide the beef mixture among the circles, brush the edges with water, fold in half, and press with a fork to seal. Transfer to a baking sheet and brush with the egg. Bake until golden, 20 to 25 minutes.

▶ Place the sour cream in a bowl and sprinkle with the lime zest. Serve with the empanadas.

peanut chicken skewers with chili mayonnaise

hands-on time: 45 minutes / total time: 55 minutes
serves 8

¾ cup salted roasted peanuts, finely chopped
½ cup panko bread crumbs
¼ cup chopped fresh cilantro or flat-leaf parsley
  Kosher salt and black pepper
2 8-ounce boneless, skinless chicken breasts, cut crosswise into 24 thin strips
3 tablespoons canola oil
½ cup mayonnaise
1 to 2 teaspoons Asian chili-garlic sauce

▶ Soak 24 wooden skewers in water for 10 minutes. On a large plate, toss together the peanuts, bread crumbs, cilantro, and ½ teaspoon each salt and pepper.

▶ Thread each strip of chicken onto a skewer and coat with the peanut mixture, pressing gently to help it adhere.

▶ Heat the oil in a large nonstick skillet over medium heat. In batches, cook the skewers until golden, 2 to 3 minutes per side, adding more oil to the skillet as necessary; transfer to a plate.

▶ In a small bowl, combine the mayonnaise and chili-garlic sauce. Serve with the chicken.

double tomato crostini

hands-on time: 10 minutes / total time: 15 minutes
serves 4

12 slices baguette
 1 tablespoon olive oil
¼ cup sun-dried tomato spread
 1 cup cherry tomatoes, cut up
    Kosher salt and black pepper

▶ Heat oven to 375° F. Place the baguette slices on a baking sheet and brush both sides with the oil. Toast until golden, 10 to 12 minutes.

▶ Dividing evenly, top the toasted baguette slices with the tomato spread and tomatoes. Season with ¼ teaspoon each salt and pepper.

shrimp with ginger sauce

hands-on time: 15 minutes / total time: 15 minutes
serves 4

¾ cup apricot preserves
 1 tablespoon grated fresh ginger
    Kosher salt and black pepper
 1 pound peeled and deveined large shrimp

▶ Heat broiler. In a small saucepan, combine the preserves, ginger, and ¼ teaspoon salt. Cook over medium heat, stirring, until the preserves have melted, about 2 minutes.

▶ Place the shrimp on a foil-lined rimmed baking sheet and drizzle with half the ginger sauce; season with ¼ teaspoon each salt and pepper. Broil until browned in spots and opaque throughout, 3 to 4 minutes. Serve with the remaining sauce for dipping.

five-minute hummus

hands-on time: 5 minutes / total time: 5 minutes
serves 6 (makes 1½ cups)

1   15.5-ounce can chickpeas, rinsed
1   clove garlic
¼   cup plus 1 tablespoon olive oil
2   tablespoons fresh lemon juice
2   tablespoons tahini (sesame seed paste; optional)
1   teaspoon ground cumin
    Kosher salt
¼   teaspoon paprika
    Pitas, for serving (optional)

▶ In a food processor, puree the chickpeas, garlic, ¼ cup of the oil, lemon juice, tahini (if desired), cumin, and ¾ teaspoon salt until smooth and creamy. Add 1 to 2 tablespoons water as necessary to achieve the desired consistency.

▶ Transfer the chickpea mixture to a small bowl. Drizzle with the remaining tablespoon of oil and sprinkle with the paprika just before serving. Serve with the pitas, if desired.

turkey samosas

hands-on time: 15 minutes / total time: 50 minutes
serves 4

1   cup shredded roasted turkey or chicken
¼   cup mango chutney, plus more for serving
1   refrigerated rolled piecrust
½   cup mashed potatoes

▶ Heat oven to 375° F. In a medium bowl, combine the turkey and chutney.

▶ Cut the piecrust into 8 wedges. Dividing evenly, top the wedges with the turkey mixture and potatoes. Brush the edges with water and pinch the corners to seal.

▶ Bake the samosas until golden brown, 25 to 35 minutes. Serve with the additional chutney for dipping.

prosciutto-fennel crostini

hands-on time: 15 minutes / total time: 15 minutes
serves 8

24 thin slices baguette
 3 tablespoons olive oil
 1 small fennel bulb—quartered, cored, and
    thinly sliced
 2 tablespoons chopped fresh flat-leaf parsley
 1 tablespoon fresh lemon juice
    Kosher salt and black pepper
½ pound thinly sliced prosciutto

▶ Heat oven to 375° F. Place the baguette slices
on a baking sheet and brush both sides with
2 tablespoons of the oil. Toast until golden, 10 to
12 minutes.

▶ Meanwhile, in a small bowl, toss the fennel
and parsley with the lemon juice, the remaining
tablespoon of oil, ¼ teaspoon salt, and ⅛ teaspoon pepper.

▶ Dividing evenly, top the baguette slices with
the prosciutto and fennel mixture.

radishes with creamy ricotta

hands-on time: 5 minutes / total time: 5 minutes
serves 4

 1 cup ricotta (preferably fresh)
 1 tablespoon olive oil
    Kosher salt and black pepper
16 radishes, halved if large

▶ Place the ricotta in a small bowl, drizzle with
the oil, and season with ⅛ teaspoon each salt
and pepper. Serve with the radishes.

smoked salmon pizzettes

hands-on time: 5 minutes / total time: 30 minutes
serves 4

- 1 pound pizza dough, thawed if frozen
  Cornmeal, for the pan
- 2 shallots, sliced
- $\frac{1}{2}$ cup crème fraîche or sour cream
- 4 ounces sliced smoked salmon
- 2 tablespoons capers
- 2 tablespoons chopped fresh chives

▸ Heat oven to 425° F. Shape the dough into 4 small rounds and place on a cornmeal-dusted rimmed baking sheet.

▸ Sprinkle the dough with the shallots, pressing them in gently, and spread with the crème fraîche. Bake until golden brown, 20 to 25 minutes.

▸ Top the pizzettes with the smoked salmon and sprinkle with the capers and chives.

grilled teriyaki wings

hands-on time: 15 minutes / total time: 30 minutes
serves 4

- 8 chicken wings (about 1$\frac{1}{2}$ pounds total)
- $\frac{1}{4}$ cup teriyaki sauce, plus more for serving
- $\frac{1}{2}$ teaspoon toasted sesame seeds

▸ Heat grill to medium-low. Halve each wing through the joint; cut off and discard the wing tip.

▸ Grill the wings, covered, turning occasionally, until cooked through, 20 to 25 minutes. During the last 5 minutes of grilling, brush with the teriyaki sauce.

▸ Sprinkle the wings with the sesame seeds and serve with the additional teriyaki sauce for dipping.

caramelized onion tarts with apples

hands-on time: 20 minutes / total time: 55 minutes
serves 8

- 2 tablespoons olive oil
- 2 medium onions, sliced
- 2 red apples (such as Braeburn or Gala), cut into small pieces
  Kosher salt and black pepper
- 2 sheets frozen puff pastry (one 17.3-ounce package), thawed
- ½ cup crème fraîche or sour cream

▶ Heat oven to 400° F. Heat the oil in a large skillet over medium heat. Add the onions and cook, stirring occasionally, until golden brown and soft, 12 to 15 minutes. Add the apples, ½ teaspoon salt, and ¼ teaspoon pepper and cook until just tender, 2 minutes.

▶ Place each sheet of pastry on a parchment-lined baking sheet and prick all over with a fork. Spread with the crème fraîche, leaving a ½-inch border. Top with the onion mixture and bake until the pastry is browned and crisp, 30 to 35 minutes. Cut each tart into 12 pieces.

beef skewers with blue cheese sauce

hands-on time: 15 minutes / total time: 25 minutes
serves 4

- ½ pound flank steak
- 2 tablespoons balsamic vinegar
  Kosher salt and black pepper
- ½ cup blue cheese dressing
- 2 scallions, sliced

▶ Place the beef in the freezer for 10 minutes. Soak 16 wooden skewers in water for 10 minutes.

▶ Thinly slice the beef against the grain into 16 pieces and thread onto the skewers.

▶ Heat grill to medium-high. Brush the beef with the vinegar, season with ¼ teaspoon each salt and pepper, and grill until cooked through, 1 to 2 minutes per side.

▶ Serve the beef with the dressing, sprinkled with the scallions, for dipping.

mini grilled cheese and chutney sandwiches

hands-on time: 20 minutes / total time: 20 minutes
serves 8

12 slices white sandwich bread
12 ounces fontina or Gruyère, thinly sliced
 1 cup fruit chutney (such as cranberry, fig, or mango)
 2 tablespoons unsalted butter

▶ Form 6 sandwiches with the bread, fontina, and chutney.

▶ In 2 batches, melt the butter in a large skillet over medium heat and cook the sandwiches until the bread is golden and the fontina has melted, 2 to 3 minutes per side. Cut each sandwich into quarters before serving.

currant-glazed cocktail meatballs

hands-on time: 10 minutes / total time: 20 minutes
serves 8

 1 pound ground beef
½ small red onion, finely chopped
½ cup bread crumbs
 1 large egg
¼ teaspoon ground nutmeg
    Kosher salt and black pepper
½ cup currant jelly

▶ Heat broiler. In a medium bowl, combine the beef, onion, bread crumbs, egg, nutmeg, ½ teaspoon salt, and ¼ teaspoon pepper.

▶ Shape the meat mixture into 1-inch balls and place on a broilerproof rimmed baking sheet. Broil, turning once, until cooked through, 5 to 6 minutes.

▶ In a large skillet, heat the currant jelly until melted. Add the meatballs and gently toss to coat.

baked Camembert with sun-dried tomatoes

hands-on time: 5 minutes / total time: 20 minutes
serves 8

1. 8-ounce round Camembert (sold in a wooden box)
¼ cup sun-dried tomatoes (packed in oil), drained and sliced
2. cloves garlic, sliced
1. tablespoon fresh thyme leaves
1. tablespoon olive oil
   Bread or crackers, for serving

▶ Heat oven to 375° F. Remove the Camembert from its paper or plastic wrapping, return it to the wooden box (discard the wrapping and lid), and place it on a baking sheet.

▶ Top the Camembert with the sun-dried tomatoes, garlic, and thyme. Drizzle with the oil and bake until soft, 10 to 12 minutes. Serve immediately with the bread.

sweet pea and ricotta crostini

hands-on time: 10 minutes / total time: 20 minutes
serves 4

16. thin slices baguette
4. tablespoons olive oil
1. 10-ounce package frozen peas, thawed
½ cup ricotta
1. scallion, coarsely chopped
1. ounce Parmesan, cut into pieces, plus more, grated, for topping
   Kosher salt and black pepper

▶ Heat oven to 375° F. Place the baguette slices on a baking sheet and brush both sides with 2 tablespoons of the oil. Toast until golden, 10 to 12 minutes.

▶ Meanwhile, in a food processor, puree the peas, ricotta, scallion, and Parmesan with the remaining 2 tablespoons of oil, ½ teaspoon salt, and ¼ teaspoon pepper, scraping down the sides of the bowl occasionally, until the Parmesan has broken down and the mixture is nearly smooth.

▶ Spread the pea mixture on the toasts and sprinkle with the grated Parmesan.

mozzarella-stuffed cherry peppers

hands-on time: 15 minutes / total time: 15 minutes
serves 4

12 pickled sweet red cherry peppers (such as
     Peppadews)
 2 ounces fresh mozzarella, cut into 12 pieces
12 fresh flat-leaf parsley leaves

▶ Dividing evenly, stuff the cherry peppers with
the mozzarella and parsley.

shrimp skewers with Feta-dill sauce

hands-on time: 15 minutes / total time: 20 minutes
serves 4

2 ounces Feta, crumbled ($^1/_2$ cup)
1 tablespoon chopped fresh dill
5 tablespoons olive oil
   Kosher salt and black pepper
1 pound peeled and deveined large shrimp

▶ Soak 8 wooden skewers in water for 10 minutes. Heat grill to medium-high.

▶ In a small bowl, combine the Feta, dill, 4 tablespoons of the oil, and ⅛ teaspoon pepper.

▶ Thread the shrimp onto the skewers. Brush
with the remaining tablespoon of oil and season
with ¼ teaspoon each salt and pepper. Grill
until opaque throughout, 2 to 3 minutes per
side. Drizzle with the Feta sauce before serving.

artichoke and spinach relish with walnuts

**hands-on time: 10 minutes / total time: 15 minutes
serves 8 (makes 1½ cups)**

¼ cup walnuts
1 13.75-ounce can artichoke hearts, rinsed
   and chopped
1 cup baby spinach, chopped
¼ cup grated Parmesan (1 ounce)
3 tablespoons mayonnaise
2 tablespoons fresh lemon juice
   Kosher salt and black pepper
   Crackers and cut-up vegetables, for serving

▶ Heat oven to 400° F. Spread the walnuts on
a rimmed baking sheet and toast, tossing
occasionally, until fragrant, 6 to 8 minutes. Let
cool, then roughly chop.

▶ In a small bowl, combine the artichoke hearts,
spinach, Parmesan, mayonnaise, lemon juice,
walnuts, ¼ teaspoon salt, and ⅛ teaspoon
pepper. Serve with the crackers and vegetables.

creamy salmon spread with horseradish

**hands-on time: 10 minutes / total time: 10 minutes
serves 8 (makes 1½ cups)**

8 ounces cream cheese, at room temperature
2 tablespoons prepared horseradish
2 tablespoons chopped fresh dill
   Kosher salt and black pepper
4 ounces smoked salmon, chopped
   Crackers and cut-up vegetables, for serving

▶ In a small bowl, combine the cream cheese,
horseradish, dill, ½ teaspoon salt, and ⅛ teaspoon pepper.

▶ Fold the salmon into the cream cheese
mixture. Serve with the crackers and vegetables.

dinner tonight:
soups

black bean soup with smoky jalapeño salsa
hands-on time: 35 minutes / total time: 35 minutes / serves 4

2 tablespoons plus
   2 teaspoons olive oil
1 large poblano pepper,
   chopped
2 cloves garlic, chopped
   Kosher salt and black pepper
1 large red onion, chopped
1 teaspoon ground cumin
2 15.5-ounce cans black beans,
   rinsed
1 12-ounce bottle lager beer
3 to 4 jalapeño peppers,
   halved and seeded
½ cup fresh cilantro leaves
2 tablespoons fresh lime juice
   Tortilla chips, for serving

▶ Heat 2 tablespoons of the oil in a large saucepan over medium heat. Add the poblano, garlic, ¾ teaspoon salt, ½ teaspoon black pepper, and all but ⅓ cup of the chopped onion. Cook, stirring occasionally, until tender, 8 to 10 minutes; stir in the cumin.

▶ Heat broiler. Add the beans, beer, and ½ cup water to the saucepan. Mash some of the beans with a potato masher and bring the soup to a boil. Reduce heat and simmer, stirring occasionally, until slightly thickened, 6 to 8 minutes.

▶ Meanwhile, place the jalapeños on a broilerproof baking sheet skin-side up and broil until charred, 2 to 3 minutes.

▶ Slice the jalapeños crosswise and, in a small bowl, toss with the cilantro, lime juice, the remaining ⅓ cup of chopped onion and 2 teaspoons of oil, and ¼ teaspoon each salt and black pepper. Top the soup with the jalapeño salsa before serving with the tortilla chips.

TIP
The jalapeño salsa in this recipe really wakes up the mellow black beans. You could also serve the soup with store-bought fresh salsa.

easy shrimp bisque

hands-on time: 15 minutes / total time: 20 minutes / serves 4

1 tablespoon butter
1 pound peeled and deveined medium or large shrimp, cut into pieces
   Kosher salt and black pepper
2 tablespoons brandy
2 14.5-ounce cans tomato soup
1 cup heavy cream
1 tablespoon chopped fresh chives
   Country bread, for serving

▶ Melt the butter in a large saucepan over medium heat. Season the shrimp with ½ teaspoon salt and ¼ teaspoon pepper and cook, tossing occasionally, until opaque throughout, 3 to 4 minutes; transfer to a plate.

▶ Add the brandy to the saucepan and cook, stirring, for 1 minute. Add the tomato soup and heavy cream and simmer until slightly thickened, 4 to 5 minutes.

▶ Top the bisque with the shrimp and chives before serving with the bread.

TIP
To intensify the seafood flavor, replace ½ cup of the tomato soup with bottled clam juice.

Asian dumpling soup with shiitakes and edamame

hands-on time: 25 minutes / total time: 25 minutes / serves 4

8 cups low-sodium chicken broth
1 2-inch piece fresh ginger, peeled and thinly sliced
1 16-ounce package frozen pot sticker dumplings or Japanese gyoza
2 medium carrots, halved lengthwise and sliced
4 ounces shiitake mushrooms, stems discarded and caps thinly sliced
2 cups frozen shelled edamame
1 bunch watercress, thick stems removed (about 3 cups)
1 tablespoon low-sodium soy sauce
Kosher salt
2 scallions, sliced

▶ In a large saucepan, bring the broth and ginger to a boil. Add the dumplings and carrots and simmer until the carrots are just tender, 8 to 10 minutes.

▶ Add the mushrooms and edamame to the saucepan and simmer until heated through, about 2 minutes.

▶ Add the watercress, soy sauce, and ½ teaspoon salt to the saucepan and stir to combine. Sprinkle with the scallions before serving.

TIP
For an extra boost of protein, stir in cubes of firm tofu along with the mushrooms and edamame.

chicken posole

hands-on time: 10 minutes / total time: 25 minutes / serves 4

1 tablespoon olive oil
1 onion, thinly sliced
   Kosher salt and black pepper
4 cups low-sodium chicken
   broth
1 28-ounce can diced
   tomatoes, drained
1 dried ancho chili pepper,
   thinly sliced, or ¼ teaspoon
   crushed red pepper
2 cups shredded rotisserie
   chicken
1 15-ounce can hominy, rinsed
1 lime, cut into wedges

▶ Heat the oil in a large saucepan over medium heat. Add the onion and ¼ teaspoon each salt and black pepper and cook, stirring occasionally, until soft and beginning to brown, 10 to 12 minutes.

▶ Add the broth, tomatoes, and chili pepper to the saucepan and bring to a boil. Stir in the chicken and hominy and simmer until heated through, 3 to 4 minutes. Serve with the lime.

TIP
Hominy is corn kernels whose outer hull and germ have been removed. You can find it in the supermarket with other canned vegetables or in the Mexican-food aisle.

turkey and bean chili

hands-on time: 15 minutes / total time: 40 minutes / serves 4

1 tablespoon olive oil
1 onion, chopped
1 green bell pepper, chopped
2 cloves garlic, chopped
½ pound ground turkey
  (preferably dark meat)
2 tablespoons tomato paste
1 teaspoon ground cumin
½ teaspoon ground chipotle
  chili pepper or 2 teaspoons
  chili powder
1 28-ounce can diced
  tomatoes
2 15.5-ounce cans kidney
  beans, rinsed
  Kosher salt and black pepper
¼ cup reduced-fat sour cream
  Fresh cilantro sprigs

▸ Heat the oil in a large saucepan over medium-high heat. Add the onion, bell pepper, and garlic and cook, stirring occasionally, until tender, 4 to 6 minutes.

▸ Add the turkey to the saucepan and cook, breaking it up with a spoon, until no longer pink, 3 to 5 minutes. Stir in the tomato paste, cumin, and chili pepper and cook, stirring, for 1 minute more.

▸ Add the tomatoes (with their juices), beans, ½ cup water, 1¼ teaspoons salt, and ¼ teaspoon black pepper to the saucepan and bring to a boil. Reduce heat and simmer, stirring occasionally, until the chili has slightly thickened, 12 to 15 minutes. Top with the sour cream and cilantro before serving.

TIP
For added color and crunch, stir in a 10-ounce package of frozen corn toward the end of cooking.

shrimp and corn chowder with fennel

hands-on time: 30 minutes / total time: 30 minutes / serves 4

2 tablespoons unsalted butter

2 leeks (white and light green parts), chopped

1 fennel bulb, cored and chopped
  Kosher salt and black pepper

2 tablespoons all-purpose flour

3 cups whole milk

1 8-ounce bottle clam juice

1 pound Yukon gold potatoes (about 2), peeled and cut into 1/2-inch pieces

3/4 pound cooked peeled and deveined medium shrimp

1 10-ounce package frozen corn

2 tablespoons chopped fresh flat-leaf parsley

2 tablespoons fresh lemon juice
  Country bread, for serving

▶ Heat the butter in a large saucepan over medium heat. Add the leeks, fennel, ½ teaspoon salt, and ¼ teaspoon pepper and cook, stirring occasionally, until tender, 4 to 5 minutes; stir in the flour.

▶ Add the milk, clam juice, and potatoes to the saucepan and bring to a boil. Reduce heat and simmer, stirring occasionally, for 12 minutes. Stir in the shrimp and corn and cook until the potatoes are tender and the shrimp and corn are heated through, 3 to 5 minutes more. Stir in the parsley and lemon juice. Serve with the bread.

TIP
Make the soup even more of an indulgence with a bit of bacon. Cook 6 slices in a large saucepan over medium heat until crisp, then remove. Cook the leeks and fennel in the bacon drippings instead of the butter and proceed with the recipe as written. Crumble the cooked bacon over the finished chowder.

French onion soup

hands-on time: 2 hours / total time: 2 hours / serves 8

6 tablespoons unsalted butter

4 pounds onions (about
6 medium), thinly sliced
Kosher salt and black pepper

1 cup dry white wine

2 cups low-sodium beef broth

8 ½-inch-thick slices country
bread, halved crosswise
if necessary to fit serving
bowls

½ pound Gruyère or Swiss
cheese, grated (2 cups)

1 tablespoon fresh thyme
leaves

▶ Heat the butter in a large pot or Dutch oven over medium-high heat. Add the onions, 1¼ teaspoons salt, and ¼ teaspoon pepper and cook, covered, stirring occasionally, until tender, 12 to 15 minutes. Reduce heat to medium and cook, uncovered, stirring occasionally, until the onions are golden brown, 50 to 60 minutes.

▶ Add the wine to the pot and cook until slightly reduced, about 2 minutes. Add the broth and 6 cups water and bring to a boil. Reduce heat and simmer for 15 minutes.

▶ Meanwhile, heat broiler. Place the bread on a broilerproof baking sheet and broil until golden brown and crisp, 1 to 2 minutes per side. Sprinkle with the Gruyère and broil until melted, 1 to 2 minutes.

▶ Top the soup with the toasts and sprinkle with the thyme before serving.

TIP
If you have broiler-proof bowls, finish the soup the classic way: Ladle it into the bowls and set them on a rimmed baking sheet. Top the soup with the toasted bread, sprinkle with the Gruyère, and broil until melted, 2 to 3 minutes.

Tex-Mex gazpacho

hands-on time: 10 minutes / total time: 30 minutes / serves 4

2½ pounds tomatoes, chopped
2 Kirby cucumbers (about ½ pound), peeled and chopped
1 red bell pepper, chopped
1 small poblano pepper, chopped
½ small red onion, chopped
3 tablespoons fresh lime juice
2 tablespoons olive oil
Kosher salt and black pepper
⅓ cup sour cream
¼ cup pepitas (hulled roasted pumpkin seeds)
Fresh cilantro sprigs
Flour tortillas, warmed, for serving

▶ In a blender, working in batches, puree the tomatoes, cucumbers, bell and poblano peppers, and onion, transferring the pureed mixture to a large bowl as you work.

▶ Add the lime juice, oil, 1¼ teaspoons salt, and ½ teaspoon black pepper to the bowl and stir to combine. Refrigerate until chilled, 15 to 20 minutes.

▶ Top the gazpacho with the sour cream, pepitas, and cilantro before serving with the tortillas.

TIP
Store tomatoes at room temperature (away from direct sunlight)—never in the refrigerator, where the cold can prevent ripening, dull the flavor, and turn the flesh mealy.

turkey, dill, and orzo soup

hands-on time: 10 minutes / total time: 20 minutes / serves 4

6 cups low-sodium chicken
broth

4 small carrots, sliced

½ cup orzo

1½ cups shredded roasted
turkey or chicken
Kosher salt and black pepper

2 tablespoons chopped
fresh dill

▶ In a large saucepan, bring the broth to a boil. Add the carrots and orzo and simmer until tender, 12 to 15 minutes.

▶ Add the turkey and ¼ teaspoon each salt and pepper to the saucepan and simmer until heated through, 2 to 3 minutes. Sprinkle with the dill before serving.

TIP
Delicious on its own, this easy soup is also a good base for all manner of vegetables you may have on hand. Try adding potatoes, parsnips, butternut squash, green beans, spinach, or chard.

smoky fish chowder

hands-on time: 20 minutes / total time: 30 minutes / serves 8

8 ounces cured chorizo, thinly
   sliced
4 leeks (white and light green
   parts), halved lengthwise and
   sliced crosswise
1½ pounds Yukon gold potatoes
   (about 3 medium), cut into
   1-inch pieces
1 28-ounce can diced
   tomatoes
   Kosher salt and black pepper
2 pounds skinless halibut,
   cod, or striped bass fillet,
   cut into 2-inch pieces
½ cup chopped fresh flat-leaf
   parsley

▶ In a large pot or Dutch oven, cook the chorizo over medium-high heat until browned, 1 to 2 minutes. Add the leeks and cook, stirring occasionally, until beginning to soften, 3 to 4 minutes.

▶ Add the potatoes, tomatoes (with their juices), 3 cups water, ¾ teaspoon salt, and ¼ teaspoon pepper to the pot; cover and bring to a boil. Reduce heat and simmer until the potatoes are just tender, 10 to 12 minutes.

▶ Add the halibut to the pot and simmer gently until opaque throughout, 5 to 6 minutes. Stir in the parsley before serving.

TIP
Because the fish in this recipe is delicate, the chowder is best served immediately. Do not refrigerate it for more than 1 day, and don't freeze it.

kale and white bean soup

hands-on time: 25 minutes / total time: 30 minutes / serves 8

2 tablespoons olive oil

1 large onion, chopped

2 stalks celery, sliced

4 cloves garlic, chopped
Kosher salt and black pepper

2 15.5-ounce cans cannellini
beans, rinsed

1 cup small soup pasta (such
as tubettini, ditalini, or orzo)

1 bunch kale, thick stems
removed and leaves torn
(about 8 cups)

2 tablespoons chopped fresh
rosemary

2 ounces Parmesan, shaved
(1/2 cup), plus 1 piece
Parmesan rind (optional)

1 tablespoon fresh lemon juice
Country bread, for serving

▶ Heat the oil in a large pot or Dutch oven over medium-high heat. Add the onion, celery, garlic, 1½ teaspoons salt, and ½ teaspoon pepper and cook, stirring occasionally, until tender, 4 to 6 minutes.

▶ Add the beans, pasta, kale, rosemary, 8 cups water, and the Parmesan rind (if using) to the pot; cover and bring to a boil. Reduce heat and simmer until the pasta and kale are tender, 4 to 5 minutes.

▶ Remove the Parmesan rind from the pot and stir in the lemon juice. Sprinkle with the shaved Parmesan before serving with the bread.

TIP
Simmering the soup with the rind from a hunk of Parmesan infuses the broth with extra flavor. Store leftover rinds in the freezer and use when cooking soup, tomato sauce, or risotto.

dinner tonight: salads

creamy shrimp salad with endive and cucumber

hands-on time: 10 minutes / total time: 10 minutes / serves 4

¼ cup buttermilk

¼ cup sour cream

½ cup cornichons, sliced, plus
3 tablespoons of the brine
Kosher salt and black pepper

1 head Boston lettuce, torn
(about 6 cups)

2 heads endive, sliced

1 pound cooked peeled and
deveined medium shrimp

1 small English cucumber,
halved lengthwise and
thinly sliced crosswise

6 small radishes, thinly sliced

2 tablespoons chopped fresh
tarragon

▶ In a small bowl, whisk together the buttermilk, sour cream, cornichon brine, and ¼ teaspoon each salt and pepper.

▶ In a large bowl, combine the lettuce, endive, shrimp, cucumber, radishes, tarragon, and cornichons and toss with the dressing.

TIP
Tarragon, an herb commonly used in French cooking, tastes like a combination of basil and licorice. Either parsley or basil is a fine substitute in this recipe.

turkey and blue cheese salad

hands-on time: 10 minutes / total time: 10 minutes / serves 4

½ pound sliced roasted turkey
  or chicken
½ small red onion, thinly sliced
2 heads Boston lettuce, broken
  into large pieces
4 ounces blue cheese,
  crumbled (1 cup)
½ cup chopped almonds
¼ cup store-bought vinaigrette

▶ Divide the turkey, onion, lettuce, blue cheese, and almonds among bowls. Drizzle with the vinaigrette.

TIP
For a little bit
of sweetness, add
sliced apples or
pears or dried fruit,
such as cherries
or cranberries.

soba salad with chicken

hands-on time: 25 minutes / total time: 25 minutes / serves 4

8 ounces soba noodles

6 tablespoons canola oil

8 small chicken cutlets
(about 1½ pounds total)
Kosher salt and black pepper

3 tablespoons rice vinegar

3 tablespoons low-sodium
soy sauce

1 teaspoon grated fresh ginger

2 cups red cabbage, thinly
sliced

6 scallions, sliced

▶ Cook the noodles according to the package directions. Drain and run under cold water to cool.

▶ Meanwhile, heat 3 tablespoons of the oil in a large skillet over medium-high heat. Season the chicken with ½ teaspoon salt and ¼ teaspoon pepper. In batches, cook the chicken until golden brown and cooked through, about 2 minutes per side. Cut into strips.

▶ In a small bowl, whisk together the vinegar, soy sauce, ginger, and the remaining 3 tablespoons of oil.

▶ In a large bowl, combine the noodles, chicken, cabbage, and scallions and toss with the dressing.

TIP
Soba (Japanese buckwheat) noodles can usually be found in the international section of the supermarket. Whole-wheat linguine or spaghetti will also work in this recipe.

minty bulgur salad with salmon and cucumbers

hands-on time: 30 minutes / total time: 30 minutes / serves 4

1 tablespoon plus 1 teaspoon
  olive oil
1 pound skinless salmon fillet
  Kosher salt and black pepper
1 cup bulgur
2 Kirby cucumbers, halved
  lengthwise and thinly sliced
  crosswise
1 cup fresh flat-leaf parsley
  leaves
¼ cup torn fresh mint leaves
½ small red onion, thinly sliced
3 tablespoons fresh lemon juice

▶ Heat 1 teaspoon of the oil in a large nonstick skillet over medium heat. Season the salmon with ¼ teaspoon each salt and pepper and cook until opaque throughout, 4 to 6 minutes per side. Transfer to a plate and refrigerate until cool, about 15 minutes. Using a fork, flake the salmon into large pieces.

▶ Meanwhile, in a large bowl, combine the bulgur with 2 cups boiling water. Let stand until tender, about 25 minutes.

▶ Drain the bulgur and return it to the bowl. Add the cucumbers, parsley, mint, and onion and toss with the lemon juice, the remaining tablespoon of oil, ½ teaspoon salt, and ¼ teaspoon pepper. Gently fold in the salmon.

TIP
Made from steamed, dried, and cracked wheat, bulgur has a nutty flavor and a grainy texture that make it great for salads (think tabbouleh). If you like, substitute wild or brown rice, barley, or couscous, cooked according to the package directions.

romaine salad with turkey and manchego

hands-on time: 15 minutes / total time: 15 minutes / serves 4

¼ cup olive oil

3 tablespoons fresh lime juice

½ teaspoon ground cumin
  Kosher salt and black pepper

2 medium carrots, grated
  (about 1 cup)

¼ pound raw green beans,
  sliced crosswise

4 scallions, sliced

1 head romaine lettuce, torn

¾ pound sliced roasted turkey
  or chicken

4 ounces manchego, sliced

▸ In a medium bowl, whisk together the oil, lime juice, cumin, ½ teaspoon salt, and ¼ teaspoon pepper. Add the carrots, green beans, and scallions and toss to coat.

▸ Divide the lettuce, turkey, and manchego among bowls and serve with the carrot mixture.

TIP
To make this salad to go, roll it in a sandwich wrap or a flour tortilla.

spinach, shrimp, and avocado salad

hands-on time: 15 minutes / total time: 15 minutes / serves 4

3 tablespoons fresh lemon
  juice
3 tablespoons olive oil
1 tablespoon chopped capers
½ teaspoon honey
  Kosher salt and black pepper
2 bunches flat-leaf spinach,
  thick stems removed
  (about 8 cups)
1 pound cooked peeled and
  deveined medium shrimp
4 plum tomatoes, chopped
1 avocado, sliced

▶ In a small bowl, whisk together the lemon juice, oil, capers, honey, ½ teaspoon salt, and ¼ teaspoon pepper.

▶ In a large bowl, combine the spinach, shrimp, tomatoes, and avocado and toss with the vinaigrette.

TIP
To prepare an avocado easily, slice into it lengthwise all the way around and twist to separate the halves. Strike the pit with the blade of a chef's knife and twist to remove. Using a large spoon, scoop out the flesh from each half. Place cut-side down on a cutting board and thinly slice.

romaine salad with tomatoes and bacon

hands-on time: 15 minutes / total time: 15 minutes
serves 4

- 4 slices bacon
- ¼ cup olive oil
- ¼ cup grated Parmesan (1 ounce)
- 2 tablespoons sour cream
- 1 tablespoon white wine vinegar
  Kosher salt and black pepper
- 1 head romaine lettuce, cut into strips (about 6 cups)
- 1 cup grape tomatoes, halved
- 4 scallions, sliced

▶ In a skillet, cook the bacon over medium heat until crisp, 6 to 8 minutes. Transfer to a paper towel–lined plate. Break into pieces when cool.

▶ In a small bowl, whisk together the oil, Parmesan, sour cream, vinegar, 2 tablespoons water, and ⅛ teaspoon each salt and pepper.

▶ In a large bowl, combine the lettuce, tomatoes, scallions, and bacon and toss with the dressing.

mesclun salad with chickpeas and dried cherries

hands-on time: 10 minutes / total time: 10 minutes
serves 4

- 3 tablespoons olive oil
- 2 tablespoons balsamic vinegar
- 1 teaspoon Dijon mustard
  Kosher salt and black pepper
- 6 ounces mesclun (about 6 cups)
- 2 carrots, halved lengthwise and thinly sliced on the bias
- 1 15.5-ounce can chickpeas, rinsed
- ½ cup dried cherries
- ¼ cup fresh dill sprigs

▶ In a small bowl, whisk together the oil, vinegar, mustard, ¼ teaspoon salt, and ⅛ teaspoon pepper.

▶ In a large bowl, combine the mesclun, carrots, chickpeas, cherries, and dill and toss with the dressing.

arugula salad with green beans and radishes

hands-on time: 10 minutes / total time: 10 minutes
serves 4

¼ cup olive oil
¼ cup grated Parmesan (1 ounce)
2 tablespoons sour cream
1 tablespoon white wine vinegar
   Kosher salt and black pepper
1 large bunch arugula (about 6 cups)
1 small fennel bulb, cored and very thinly sliced
¼ pound raw green beans, cut into 1-inch pieces
   (about 1¼ cups)
6 radishes, cut into wedges

▶ In a small bowl, whisk together the oil, Parmesan, sour cream, vinegar, 2 tablespoons water, and ⅛ teaspoon each salt and pepper.

▶ In a large bowl, combine the arugula, fennel, green beans, and radishes and toss with the dressing.

watercress salad with beets and Feta

hands-on time: 10 minutes / total time: 10 minutes
serves 4

2 tablespoons olive oil
2 tablespoons fresh lemon juice
1 teaspoon honey
½ shallot, finely chopped
   Kosher salt and black pepper
2 bunches watercress, thick stems removed
   (about 6 cups)
1 15-ounce can whole beets, drained and thinly sliced
2 ounces Feta, crumbled (½ cup)

▶ In a small bowl, whisk together the oil, lemon juice, honey, shallot, ¼ teaspoon salt, and ⅛ teaspoon pepper.

▶ In a large bowl, combine the watercress and beets and toss with the dressing. Sprinkle with the Feta.

Moroccan chicken salad with carrots

hands-on time: 20 minutes / total time: 20 minutes / serves 4

5 tablespoons olive oil

8 small chicken cutlets (about 1½ pounds total)

1 teaspoon ground cumin
Kosher salt and black pepper

3 tablespoons fresh lime juice

¼ teaspoon crushed red pepper

5 ounces baby spinach (about 6 cups)

2 cups fresh cilantro leaves

4 carrots, peeled into strips with a vegetable peeler

½ cup raisins

▶ Heat 2 tablespoons of the oil in a large skillet over medium-high heat. Season the chicken with the cumin, ½ teaspoon salt, and ¼ teaspoon black pepper. In batches, cook the chicken until golden brown and cooked through, about 2 minutes per side. Cut into strips.

▶ In a small bowl, whisk together the lime juice, red pepper, the remaining 3 tablespoons of oil, and ½ teaspoon salt.

▶ In a large bowl, combine the spinach, chicken, cilantro, carrots, and raisins and toss with the dressing.

TIP
To make this easy recipe even faster, substitute shredded rotisserie chicken for the cooked cutlets.

grilled salmon salad with grapefruit

hands-on time: 20 minutes / total time: 20 minutes / serves 4

4 6-ounce pieces skinless
   salmon fillet
   Kosher salt and black pepper
1 grapefruit
4 cups mixed greens
1 avocado, diced
¼ small red onion, sliced
2 tablespoons olive oil
2 teaspoons red wine vinegar

▶ Heat grill to medium. Season the salmon with ½ teaspoon salt and ¼ teaspoon pepper and grill until opaque throughout, 5 to 6 minutes per side. Transfer to a plate and refrigerate for 5 minutes. Using a fork, flake the salmon into large pieces.

▶ Meanwhile, cut away the peel and pith of the grapefruit. Working over a large bowl, cut along the membranes between segments to release them, adding them to the bowl as you go.

▶ Add the greens, avocado, and onion to the bowl and gently toss with the oil, vinegar, and ¼ teaspoon each salt and pepper. Serve the salad topped with the salmon.

TIP
Instead of grilling the salmon, you can cook it in 1 table-spoon of oil in a large skillet over medium heat until opaque throughout, 5 to 6 minutes per side.

Asian beef and cabbage salad

hands-on time: 25 minutes / total time: 25 minutes / serves 4

4 tablespoons canola oil
1 pound ground beef
¼ cup plum sauce
⅓ cup rice vinegar
   Kosher salt and black pepper
4 cups shredded Napa cabbage
2 large carrots, cut into
   thin strips
1 cup fresh cilantro leaves
4 scallions, sliced

▶ Heat 1 tablespoon of the oil in a large skillet over medium-high heat. Add the beef and cook, breaking it up with a spoon, until browned, 5 to 6 minutes. Stir in the plum sauce.

▶ Meanwhile, in a small bowl, whisk together the vinegar, the remaining 3 tablespoons of oil, ½ teaspoon salt, and ¼ teaspoon pepper.

▶ In a large bowl, combine the cabbage, carrots, cilantro, and scallions and toss with the dressing. Serve with the beef.

TIP
For variety, try this recipe with ground turkey or pork.

Caesar salad with grilled chicken and garlic

hands-on time: 20 minutes / total time: 20 minutes / serves 4

2 tablespoons plus
   2 teaspoons olive oil
1 head garlic, cloves separated,
   unpeeled
4 6-ounce boneless, skinless
   chicken breasts
   Kosher salt and black pepper
½ baguette, cut into ½-inch-
   thick slices
2 anchovy fillets, finely
   chopped
2 tablespoons fresh lemon juice
1 tablespoon Dijon mustard
½ teaspoon Worcestershire
   sauce
2 hearts of romaine lettuce,
   quartered lengthwise
2 ounces Parmesan, shaved
   (½ cup)

▶ Heat grill to medium-high. Place 1 teaspoon of the oil and all but 2 cloves of the garlic on a piece of heavy-duty foil. Fold over the foil and seal the edges to form a pouch. Grill, shaking occasionally, until the garlic is soft, 10 to 12 minutes.

▶ Meanwhile, rub the chicken with 1 teaspoon of the remaining oil and season with ¼ teaspoon each salt and pepper. Grill the chicken until cooked through, 5 to 6 minutes per side. Grill the baguette slices until crisp, about 1 minute per side.

▶ Peel and finely chop the remaining 2 garlic cloves. In a large bowl, combine them with the anchovies, lemon juice, mustard, Worcestershire, and the remaining 2 tablespoons of oil. Add the lettuce and toss to combine.

▶ Serve the salad with the chicken and sprinkle with the Parmesan. Squeeze the grilled garlic cloves from their skins and serve with the grilled bread.

TIP
The anchovies give this dressing a rich, salty—not fishy— flavor. But omit them if you prefer.

chopped steak salad

hands-on time: 15 minutes / total time: 15 minutes / serves 4

¾ pound flank steak
  Kosher salt and black pepper
1 head romaine lettuce,
  chopped
2 cups chopped red cabbage
1 15.5-ounce can cannellini
  beans, rinsed
½ cup chopped roasted
  red peppers
¼ cup chopped fresh flat-
  leaf parsley
¼ cup store-bought vinaigrette

▸ Heat broiler. Season the steak with ½ teaspoon salt and ¼ teaspoon black pepper and place on a broiler-proof rimmed baking sheet.

▸ Broil the steak to the desired doneness, 4 to 5 minutes per side for medium-rare. Let rest for 5 minutes, then cut into small pieces.

▸ Meanwhile, in a large bowl, combine the lettuce, cabbage, beans, roasted red peppers, parsley, and steak and toss with the vinaigrette.

TIP
This salad is a tasty way to use up leftover steak (or lamb or pork) from last night's dinner.

Mediterranean salad with shrimp and chickpeas

hands-on time: 15 minutes / total time: 15 minutes / serves 4

½ head romaine lettuce, cut into thin strips
1 pound cooked peeled and deveined medium shrimp, halved crosswise
½ English cucumber, chopped
1 15.5-ounce can chickpeas, rinsed
½ sweet onion, chopped
3 ounces Feta, crumbled (¾ cup)
½ cup pitted kalamata olives, halved
2 cups pita chips
3 tablespoons olive oil
2 tablespoons red wine vinegar
Kosher salt and black pepper

▶ In a large bowl, combine the lettuce, shrimp, cucumber, chickpeas, onion, Feta, and olives. Crumble the pita chips into the salad.

▶ Add the oil, vinegar, and ¼ teaspoon each salt and pepper to the salad and toss to combine.

TIP
In place of the chickpeas, use any other mild white beans, such as cannellini, navy, great Northern, or butter beans.

turkey Waldorf salad

hands-on time: 5 minutes / total time: 10 minutes / serves 4

2 tablespoons sour cream
2 tablespoons mayonnaise
1 tablespoon white wine vinegar
  Kosher salt and black pepper
1 cup shredded roasted turkey
  or chicken
1 celery stalk, sliced
1 Granny Smith apple, cut into
  ¹/₂-inch pieces
2 tablespoons chopped toasted
  walnuts
1 small head red leaf lettuce,
  torn

▶ In a medium bowl, whisk together the sour cream, mayonnaise, vinegar, ½ teaspoon salt, and ¼ teaspoon pepper. Add the turkey, celery, apple, and walnuts and toss to combine.

▶ Divide the lettuce among bowls and top with the turkey mixture.

TIP
To toast walnuts, spread them on a rimmed baking sheet and cook in a 350° F oven, tossing occasionally, until fragrant, 8 to 10 minutes.

dinner tonight:
poultry

braised chicken and spring vegetables

hands-on time: 15 minutes / total time: 40 minutes / serves 4

1 tablespoon olive oil
8 small bone-in chicken thighs
  (about 2½ pounds total)
  Kosher salt and black pepper
1 cup low-sodium chicken broth
12 medium radishes, halved
¾ pound carrots (about 4),
  cut into sticks
1 teaspoon sugar
2 tablespoons chopped fresh
  chives

▶ Heat the oil in a Dutch oven over medium-high heat. Season the chicken with ½ teaspoon salt and ¼ teaspoon pepper and cook until browned, 6 to 7 minutes per side; transfer to a plate.

▶ Spoon off and discard the fat. Return the pot to medium-high heat, add the broth, and scrape up any brown bits.

▶ Add the radishes, carrots, and sugar to the pot. Place the chicken on top of the vegetables and gently simmer, partially covered, until it is cooked through, 15 to 20 minutes. Sprinkle with the chives.

TIP
Patience is key when browning chicken. It's ready to be turned when it releases easily from the pan (don't tug). Turn it too soon and you interrupt the caramelizing process and risk tearing the skin.

Havarti-stuffed chicken breasts with tomato salad

hands-on time: 20 minutes / total time: 20 minutes / serves 4

4 6-ounce boneless, skinless chicken breasts

4 ounces dill Havarti, cut into small pieces
  Kosher salt and black pepper

3 tablespoons olive oil

1 pound heirloom tomatoes, sliced

4 pepperoncini peppers, thinly sliced

▶ Cut a 2-inch pocket in the thickest part of each chicken breast. Dividing evenly, stuff the pockets with the Havarti. Season the chicken with ½ teaspoon salt and ¼ teaspoon black pepper.

▶ Heat 1 tablespoon of the oil in a large skillet over medium-high heat. Cook the chicken until golden brown and cooked through, 6 to 8 minutes per side.

▶ Serve the chicken with the tomatoes and pepperoncini. Drizzle the vegetables with the remaining 2 tablespoons of oil and season with ½ teaspoon salt and ¼ teaspoon black pepper.

TIP
Don't overstuff the chicken breasts or press down on them during cooking. The cheese will drip into the skillet, making cooking difficult and cleanup messy.

crispy turkey cutlets with green bean salad

hands-on time: 25 minutes / total time: 25 minutes / serves 4

¾ pound green beans, trimmed
1 cup grape tomatoes, halved
½ cup pitted kalamata olives, quartered
1 tablespoon fresh lemon juice, plus lemon wedges for serving
4 tablespoons olive oil
Kosher salt and black pepper
¼ cup all-purpose flour
2 large eggs, beaten
⅔ cup bread crumbs
4 thin turkey cutlets (about 1 pound total)

▶ In a large saucepan fitted with a steamer basket, bring 1 inch of water to a boil. Place the green beans in the basket, cover, and steam until tender, 4 to 5 minutes. Run under cold water to cool.

▶ In a large bowl, toss the green beans, tomatoes, and olives with the lemon juice, 1 tablespoon of the oil, and ¼ teaspoon each salt and pepper.

▶ Place the flour, eggs, and bread crumbs in separate shallow bowls. Season the turkey with ½ teaspoon salt and ¼ teaspoon pepper. Coat with the flour (tapping off any excess), dip in the eggs (shaking off any excess), then coat with the bread crumbs, pressing gently to help them adhere.

▶ Heat the remaining 3 tablespoons of oil in a large skillet over medium-high heat. Cook the turkey until golden and cooked through, 2 to 3 minutes per side. Serve with the salad and lemon wedges.

TIP
The green beans can be cooked and the cutlets breaded up to a day in advance; refrigerate, covered, separately. Cook the cutlets and finish the salad just before serving.

Thai red curry chicken

hands-on time: 20 minutes / total time: 20 minutes / serves 4

1 cup long-grain white rice
2 tablespoons canola oil
8 small chicken cutlets (about
    1½ pounds total)
    Kosher salt and black pepper
2 red bell peppers, sliced
2 tablespoons red curry paste
1 15-ounce can coconut milk
1 lime, cut into wedges
¼ cup torn fresh basil leaves

▶ Cook the rice according to the package directions.

▶ Meanwhile, heat the oil in a large skillet over medium-high heat. Season the chicken with ½ teaspoon salt and ¼ teaspoon black pepper. In batches, cook the chicken until golden brown and cooked through, 2 to 3 minutes per side; remove from the skillet and cut into strips.

▶ Add the bell peppers and ¼ cup water to the skillet and cook, tossing frequently, until just tender, 3 to 4 minutes. Add the curry paste and coconut milk and simmer until slightly thickened, 3 to 5 minutes. Add the chicken and toss to combine.

▶ Serve the chicken curry over the rice with the lime wedges and sprinkle with the basil.

TIP
Canola oil has a neutral taste and a high smoke point (meaning it can get very hot without burning). This makes it a good choice for Asian stir-fries.

roasted chicken with tomatoes and olives

hands-on time: 10 minutes / total time: 1 hour / serves 4

1 lemon
2 pints grape tomatoes
1 head garlic, cloves separated, unpeeled
1 cup pitted kalamata olives, halved
8 sprigs fresh thyme
2 tablespoons olive oil
1 3-pound chicken, cut into 8 pieces
Kosher salt and black pepper
½ cup dry white wine

▶ Heat oven to 425° F. Using a vegetable peeler, remove strips of zest from the lemon. (Reserve the lemon.)

▶ In a large roasting pan, toss the tomatoes, garlic, olives, thyme, and lemon zest with 1 tablespoon of the oil.

▶ Nestle the chicken, skin-side up, in the tomato mixture and rub with the remaining tablespoon of oil. Season with ¾ teaspoon salt and ½ teaspoon pepper and roast until the chicken is cooked through, 35 to 40 minutes. Transfer the chicken to a platter.

▶ Squeeze the lemon into the hot roasting pan and add the wine. Gently stir, scraping up any bits stuck to the pan. Serve the chicken with the tomato mixture and pan juices.

TIP
Looking for a dry white wine for cooking? Try Sauvignon Blanc, Pinot Grigio, or Chablis. Avoid "cooking wines" sold in supermarkets. Don't cook with anything that you wouldn't drink.

chicken, ham, and Swiss roulades

hands-on time: 20 minutes / total time: 30 minutes / serves 4

8 small chicken cutlets (about
    1½ pounds total)
    Kosher salt and black pepper
8 thin slices cooked ham
8 thin slices Swiss cheese
4 tablespoons olive oil
6 cups mixed greens
1 cup grape tomatoes, halved
1 tablespoon white wine
    vinegar
¼ cup whole-grain mustard

▶ Heat oven to 400° F. Season the chicken with ½ tea-spoon salt and ¼ teaspoon pepper. Roll up each cutlet with 1 slice of the ham and 1 slice of the Swiss cheese. Skewer the roulades closed with toothpicks.

▶ Heat 2 tablespoons of the oil in a large ovenproof skillet over medium-high heat. Add the roulades and cook, turning occasionally, until golden brown, 4 to 6 minutes. Transfer the skillet to oven and roast the roulades until cooked through, 8 to 10 minutes.

▶ Meanwhile, in a large bowl, toss the greens and tomatoes with the vinegar, the remaining 2 table-spoons of oil, and ¼ teaspoon each salt and pepper. Serve with the roulades and mustard.

TIP
The roulades can be prepared (but not cooked) up to a day in advance; refrigerate, covered.

chicken with spinach and mushrooms

hands-on time: 20 minutes / total time: 25 minutes / serves 4

2 tablespoons olive oil

4 6-ounce boneless, skinless chicken breasts
   Kosher salt and black pepper

1 pound button mushrooms, quartered

1 red bell pepper, cut into ½-inch pieces

2 cloves garlic, chopped

½ cup dry white wine

2 bunches flat-leaf spinach, thick stems removed (about 8 cups)

▶ Heat 1 tablespoon of the oil in a large skillet over medium-high heat. Season the chicken with ½ teaspoon salt and ¼ teaspoon black pepper. Cook until browned and cooked through, 5 to 7 minutes per side; transfer to plates.

▶ Return the skillet to medium-high heat and heat the remaining tablespoon of oil. Cook the mushrooms and bell pepper, tossing, for 3 minutes. Add the garlic and wine and cook until the mushrooms are tender and the wine is nearly evaporated, 2 to 3 minutes more.

▶ Add the spinach and ½ teaspoon each salt and black pepper to the vegetables and toss to combine. Serve with the chicken.

TIP
For even richer flavor, cook 2 slices of bacon (cut into pieces) in the skillet before adding the mushrooms and bell pepper.

roasted chicken with carrots and potatoes

hands-on time: 25 minutes / total time: 1¹/₂ hours / serves 4

1¹/₂ pounds new potatoes
 (about 20)
1 pound medium carrots
 (about 6), halved lengthwise
 and cut into 2-inch pieces
2 tablespoons olive oil
 Kosher salt and black pepper
1 lemon
8 sprigs fresh thyme
1 3¹/₂- to 4-pound chicken,
 patted dry
2 tablespoons unsalted butter,
 at room temperature

▶ Heat oven to 425° F. Place the potatoes and carrots in a large roasting pan or baking dish and toss with the oil, ½ teaspoon salt, and ¼ teaspoon pepper.

▶ Pierce the lemon several times with a knife and place it and the thyme in the cavity of the chicken. Rub the chicken with the butter and season with ½ teaspoon salt and ¼ teaspoon pepper. Tie the legs together with kitchen twine, if desired, and nestle the chicken in the vegetables.

▶ Roast until the vegetables are tender, the chicken is golden brown, and its juices run clear when the thigh is pierced with a fork, 65 to 75 minutes (an instant-read thermometer should register 165° F when inserted in the thickest part of the thigh). Let the chicken rest for at least 10 minutes before carving. Serve with the vegetables.

TIP
Find carving a bird a challenge? Use kitchen shears instead of a knife.

turkey Reubens

hands-on time: 15 minutes / total time: 15 minutes / serves 4

8 slices rye bread
2 tablespoons Dijon mustard
2 tablespoons store-bought Russian dressing
8 slices roasted turkey
1 cup sauerkraut
8 slices Swiss cheese
1 tablespoon olive oil
  Potato chips and pickles (optional)

▶ Spread 4 slices of the bread with the mustard and spread 4 slices with the Russian dressing.

▶ Dividing evenly, top the mustard-spread slices with the turkey, sauerkraut, and Swiss cheese, then the remaining slices of bread.

▶ Heat the oil in a large skillet over medium heat. Cook the sandwiches until the bread is golden brown and crisp and the cheese has melted, 3 to 4 minutes per side. Serve with the potato chips and pickles, if desired.

TIP
To make your own Russian dressing, stir together equal parts mayonnaise and ketchup.

chicken and pepper stew with olives

hands-on time: 30 minutes / total time: 1 hour / serves 8

½ cup all-purpose flour
1 teaspoon paprika (preferably smoked)
Kosher salt and black pepper
3 tablespoons olive oil
16 boneless, skinless chicken thighs (about 6 pounds total), halved
3 red bell peppers, sliced
3 green bell peppers, sliced
4 cloves garlic, smashed
2 cups low-sodium chicken broth
2 cups pitted olives
½ cup golden raisins
2 cups long-grain white rice

▸ In a large bowl, combine the flour, paprika, 1 teaspoon salt, and ½ teaspoon black pepper.

▸ Heat 1 tablespoon of the oil in a large pot or Dutch oven over medium-high heat. Coat the chicken with the flour mixture (tapping off any excess). In batches, cook the chicken until browned, turning occasionally, 6 to 8 minutes. Transfer to a plate and add the remaining 2 tablespoons of oil.

▸ Add the bell peppers, garlic, ½ cup of the broth, ½ teaspoon salt, and ¼ teaspoon black pepper to the pot. Cook, stirring and scraping up any browned bits, until the bell peppers begin to soften, 4 to 6 minutes.

▸ Add the olives, raisins, and the remaining 1½ cups of broth to the pot and bring to a boil. Nestle the chicken in the vegetables and simmer, covered, for 15 minutes. Uncover and simmer until the chicken is cooked through and the sauce is slightly thickened, 15 to 20 minutes more.

▸ Twenty minutes before the stew is done, cook the rice according to the package directions. Serve with the stew.

TIP
The stew can be refrigerated, covered, for up to 2 days or frozen for up to 3 months.

grilled lemon chicken with cabbage and corn slaw

hands-on time: 20 minutes / total time: 20 minutes / serves 4

2 teaspoons honey

2 tablespoons plus 1 teaspoon olive oil

5 tablespoons fresh lemon juice
Kosher salt and black pepper

¼ small green cabbage (about ½ pound), cored and thinly sliced

1 red bell pepper, thinly sliced

1 cup corn kernels (from 1 to 2 ears, or thawed if frozen)

4 6-ounce boneless, skinless chicken breasts

▶ In a large bowl, whisk together the honey, 2 tablespoons of the oil, 2 tablespoons of the lemon juice, ½ teaspoon salt, and ¼ teaspoon black pepper. Add the cabbage, bell pepper, and corn and toss to combine.

▶ Heat grill to medium-high. Rub the chicken with the remaining teaspoon of oil and season with ½ teaspoon each salt and black pepper. Grill the chicken, basting often with the remaining 3 tablespoons of lemon juice, until cooked through, 5 to 6 minutes per side. Serve with the slaw.

TIP
For a lighter, more delicate take on this summery slaw, substitute Napa cabbage for the common variety.

chicken with creamy mushrooms

hands-on time: 20 minutes / total time: 20 minutes / serves 4

3 tablespoons olive oil

8 small chicken cutlets
(1$\frac{1}{2}$ pounds total)
Kosher salt and black pepper

1 pound button mushrooms,
sliced

$\frac{1}{2}$ cup heavy cream

2 ounces fresh goat cheese,
crumbled ($\frac{1}{2}$ cup)

$\frac{1}{4}$ cup chopped fresh flat-leaf
parsley

▶ Heat 2 tablespoons of the oil in a large skillet over medium-high heat. Season the chicken with $\frac{1}{2}$ teaspoon salt and $\frac{1}{4}$ teaspoon pepper. In batches, cook until golden brown, 2 to 3 minutes per side; transfer to plates.

▶ Add the mushrooms and the remaining tablespoon of oil to the skillet and cook, tossing occasionally, until tender, 4 to 5 minutes. Stir in the heavy cream, goat cheese, parsley, and $\frac{1}{4}$ teaspoon each salt and pepper. Serve over the chicken.

TIP
For richer flavor and a prettier presentation, try mixed wild mushrooms (often sold as a packaged assortment) in place of the button variety in this recipe.

spicy orange-glazed drumsticks with green beans

hands-on time: 15 minutes / total time: 45 minutes / serves 4

¼ cup orange marmalade
½ teaspoon Asian chili-garlic
  sauce
8 chicken drumsticks (about
  2½ pounds total)
  Kosher salt and black pepper
1 pound green beans, trimmed
1 tablespoon unsalted butter
4 corn muffins, warmed

▶ Heat oven to 400° F. In a small bowl, combine the marmalade and chili-garlic sauce.

▶ Place the chicken on a foil-lined rimmed baking sheet and season with ½ teaspoon salt and ¼ teaspoon pepper. Roast until cooked through, 35 to 40 minutes, brushing occasionally with the marmalade mixture during the last 10 minutes of cooking.

▶ Meanwhile, bring a pot of salted water to a boil. Cook the green beans until tender, 4 to 6 minutes. Drain and toss with the butter and ¼ teaspoon each salt and pepper. Serve with the chicken and muffins.

TIP
If you don't have orange marmalade, use apricot preserves or apple jelly instead.

chicken and chorizo tostadas

hands-on time: 15 minutes / total time: 15 minutes / serves 4

1 tablespoon olive oil

4 small chicken cutlets
(about ³/₄ pound total)
Kosher salt and black pepper

4 small flour tortillas

4 ounces cured chorizo, thinly
sliced

8 ounces Cheddar, grated
(2 cups)

¹/₄ cup fresh cilantro leaves

¹/₄ cup sour cream

▶ Heat broiler. Heat the oil in a large skillet over medium-high heat. Season the chicken with ½ teaspoon salt and ¼ teaspoon pepper and cook until golden brown and cooked through, 2 to 3 minutes per side. Cut into strips.

▶ Place the tortillas on a broilerproof rimmed baking sheet and broil until crisp, about 1 minute. Dividing evenly, top with the chicken, chorizo, and Cheddar. Broil until the cheese melts. Sprinkle with the cilantro and serve with the sour cream.

TIP
Cured chorizo, also called Spanish chorizo, is a flavorful pork sausage seasoned with garlic and paprika. Try it in stews, omelets, or seafood pilafs.

chicken with shallots and mashed sweet potatoes

hands-on time: 30 minutes / total time: 30 minutes / serves 4

1½ pounds sweet potatoes,
   (about 3), peeled and cut
   into 2-inch pieces
   Kosher salt and black pepper
4 tablespoons olive oil
4 6-ounce boneless, skinless
   chicken breasts
4 shallots, sliced into thin rings
2 tablespoons roughly
   chopped fresh rosemary

▶ Place the sweet potatoes in a large pot and add enough cold water to cover. Bring to a boil and add 1 teaspoon salt. Reduce heat and simmer until tender, 14 to 16 minutes. Reserve ¼ cup of the cooking water, drain the sweet potatoes, and return them to the pot. Mash with the reserved cooking water.

▶ Meanwhile, heat 1 tablespoon of the oil in a large skillet over medium heat. Season the chicken with ½ teaspoon salt and ¼ teaspoon pepper and cook until golden brown and cooked through, 7 to 8 minutes per side; transfer to plates.

▶ Wipe out the skillet and heat the remaining 3 tablespoons of oil over medium-high heat. Add the shallots, rosemary, ½ teaspoon salt, and ¼ teaspoon pepper and cook, stirring, until the shallots are tender, 3 to 4 minutes. Serve the chicken with the potatoes and top with the shallot mixture.

TIP
Mashing the sweet potatoes with some of their cooking water is a healthy, low-fat alternative to using butter, cream, or milk. Try the same technique with white potatoes.

baked chicken Parmesan

hands-on time: 15 minutes / total time: 40 minutes / serves 4

¼ cup all-purpose flour
2 large eggs, beaten
⅔ cup bread crumbs
¼ cup grated Parmesan
   (1 ounce)
8 small chicken cutlets
   (1½ pounds total)
   Kosher salt and black pepper
3 tablespoons olive oil
1 24-ounce jar marinara sauce
1 pound fresh mozzarella,
   sliced

▸ Heat oven to 400° F. Place the flour and eggs in separate shallow bowls. In a third shallow bowl, combine the bread crumbs and Parmesan. Season the chicken with ½ teaspoon salt and ¼ teaspoon pepper. Coat with the flour (tapping off any excess), dip in the eggs (shaking off any excess), then coat with the bread crumb mixture, pressing gently to help it adhere.

▸ Heat the oil in a large skillet over medium-high heat. In batches, cook the chicken until golden brown, 2 to 3 minutes per side; transfer to a plate.

▸ Pour the marinara sauce into a large, shallow baking dish. Nestle the chicken in the sauce and top with the mozzarella. Bake until the cheese is bubbling and golden brown, 20 to 25 minutes.

TIP
Add extra crunch to this kid-approved dish by coating the cutlets in Japanese-style panko bread crumbs.

spiced chicken with couscous salad

hands-on time: 10 minutes / total time: 25 minutes / serves 4

3 tablespoons olive oil

4 6-ounce boneless, skinless chicken breasts

1 tablespoon paprika

2 teaspoons ground cumin
   Kosher salt and black pepper

¾ cup couscous

¾ pound cherry or grape tomatoes, quartered

¼ pound snap peas, thinly sliced crosswise (about 1 cup)

½ cup torn fresh basil leaves

½ teaspoon grated lemon zest plus 2 tablespoons fresh lemon juice

▶ Heat 1 tablespoon of the oil in a large skillet over medium heat. Season the chicken with the paprika, cumin, ½ teaspoon salt, and ¼ teaspoon pepper. Cook until browned and cooked through, 6 to 7 minutes per side. Let the chicken rest for at least 5 minutes before slicing.

▶ Meanwhile, place the couscous in a large bowl. Add 1 cup hot tap water, cover, and let sit for 5 minutes; fluff with a fork. Add the tomatoes, snap peas, basil, lemon zest and juice, the remaining 2 tablespoons of oil, ½ teaspoon salt, and ¼ teaspoon pepper and toss to combine. Serve with the chicken.

TIP
No need to spend time removing the strings from the snap peas for this salad. Cutting the peas into small pieces will keep the fibers from being a nuisance.

chicken with fennel-orange salad

hands-on time: 20 minutes / total time: 20 minutes / serves 4

4 tablespoons olive oil

8 small chicken cutlets (about
1½ pounds total)

1 teaspoon ground coriander
Kosher salt and black pepper

1 fennel bulb, cored and thinly
sliced

1 cup fresh flat-leaf parsley
leaves

1 tablespoon white wine
vinegar

2 oranges, segmented

▶ Heat 2 tablespoons of the oil in a large skillet over medium-high heat. Season the chicken with the coriander, ½ teaspoon salt, and ¼ teaspoon pepper. In batches, cook the chicken until golden brown and cooked through, 2 to 3 minutes per side.

▶ In a medium bowl, toss the fennel and parsley with the vinegar, the remaining 2 tablespoons of oil, and ¼ teaspoon each salt and pepper. Fold in the oranges and serve with the chicken.

TIP
To segment an orange, use a sharp knife to cut off the top and bottom of the orange, cut away the remaining peel and white pith, then cut along the membranes between the segments to release them.

chicken with broccoli rabe, apricots, and pine nuts

hands-on time: 25 minutes / total time: 25 minutes / serves 4

1 tablespoon plus 2 teaspoons olive oil

4 6-ounce boneless, skinless chicken breasts
    Kosher salt and black pepper

6 dried apricots, sliced

2 tablespoons pine nuts

2 cloves garlic, sliced

1 bunch broccoli rabe (about 1 pound), trimmed

▶ Heat 2 teaspoons of the oil in a large skillet over medium heat. Season the chicken with ¼ teaspoon each salt and pepper and cook until golden brown and cooked through, 7 to 8 minutes per side.

▶ Meanwhile, heat the remaining tablespoon of oil in a second large skillet over medium-high heat. Add the apricots, pine nuts, and garlic and cook, stirring, until the pine nuts and garlic are golden brown, 2 to 3 minutes; remove with a slotted spoon.

▶ Add the broccoli rabe, ¼ cup water, and ½ teaspoon salt to the second skillet and cook, covered, until the broccoli rabe is tender, 2 to 3 minutes; drain. Return the apricot mixture to the skillet and toss to combine. Serve with the chicken.

TIP
If you find the peppery bite of broccoli rabe too bitter, substitute Broccolini or conventional broccoli.

crispy herbed chicken strips

hands-on time: 20 minutes / total time: 20 minutes / serves 4

¼ cup all-purpose flour
1 large egg, beaten
2 cups panko bread crumbs
¼ cup chopped fresh dill
8 small chicken cutlets
(about 1½ pounds total),
cut into wide strips
Kosher salt and black pepper
3 tablespoons olive oil
2 Kirby cucumbers, cut into
spears
½ cup store-bought ranch
dressing

▶ Place the flour and egg in separate shallow bowls. In a third shallow bowl, combine the bread crumbs and dill. Season the chicken with ½ teaspoon salt and ¼ teaspoon pepper. Coat with the flour (tapping off any excess), dip in the egg (shaking off any excess), then coat with the bread crumb mixture, pressing gently to help it adhere.

▶ Heat the oil in a skillet over medium-high heat. In batches, cook the chicken until golden brown and cooked through, 2 to 3 minutes per side. Serve with the cucumbers and dressing.

TIP
This breading method also works well with firm white fish, such as cod, halibut, or sea bass.

turkey hash with fried eggs

hands-on time: 25 minutes / total time: 25 minutes / serves 4

3 tablespoons olive oil
¾ pound red potatoes
   (about 2), cut into ¾-inch
   pieces
1 onion, chopped
1 red bell pepper, chopped
   Kosher salt and black pepper
1 cup roasted turkey, cut into
   ½-inch pieces
¼ cup chopped fresh flat-leaf
   parsley
8 large eggs

▶ Heat 2 tablespoons of the oil in a large skillet over medium heat. Add the potatoes, onion, and bell pepper and season with ½ teaspoon salt and ¼ teaspoon black pepper. Cook, stirring occasionally, until the potatoes are golden brown and tender, 12 to 15 minutes.

▶ Add the turkey and parsley to the skillet and cook, tossing occasionally, until heated through, 2 to 3 minutes more.

▶ Meanwhile, heat the remaining tablespoon of oil in a large nonstick skillet over medium heat. In 2 batches, crack the eggs into the pan and cook, covered, to the desired doneness, 2 to 4 minutes for slightly runny sunny-side-up eggs. Serve with the hash.

TIP
To add a healthy dose of green vegetables, fold chopped fresh spinach into the potatoes at the end of cooking.

chicken and prosciutto club sandwiches

hands-on time: 20 minutes / total time: 20 minutes / serves 4

8 thin slices prosciutto
1 tablespoon olive oil
4 small chicken cutlets
   (about ³/₄ pound total)
   Kosher salt and black pepper
4 sandwich rolls
¹/₄ cup mayonnaise
¹/₄ cup olive tapenade
1 medium tomato, sliced
¹/₂ cup baby arugula

▶ Heat oven to 400° F. Place the prosciutto in a single layer on a rimmed baking sheet and bake until crisp, 8 to 10 minutes.

▶ Meanwhile, heat the oil in a large skillet over medium-high heat. Season the chicken with ½ teaspoon salt and ¼ teaspoon pepper and cook until golden brown and cooked through, 2 to 3 minutes per side.

▶ Form sandwiches with the rolls, mayonnaise, tapenade, chicken, prosciutto, tomato, and arugula.

TIP
If you don't have tapenade, mix chopped black olives into the mayonnaise.

dinner tonight:
beef & lamb

grilled beef and pepper fajitas

hands-on time: 20 minutes / total time: 20 minutes / serves 4

1 pound flank steak
1 teaspoon ground cumin
  Kosher salt and black pepper
1 red bell pepper, sliced
  ½ inch thick
1 yellow bell pepper, sliced
  ½ inch thick
1 tablespoon olive oil
8 small flour tortillas
1 avocado, sliced
½ cup sour cream
  Hot sauce (optional)

▶ Heat grill to medium-high. Season the beef with the cumin, ½ teaspoon salt, and ¼ teaspoon black pepper.

▶ In a large bowl, toss the bell peppers with the oil and ¼ teaspoon each salt and black pepper.

▶ Grill the beef to the desired doneness, 4 to 5 minutes per side for medium-rare. Let rest for at least 5 minutes before slicing.

▶ Meanwhile, grill the peppers, turning occasionally, until tender, 8 to 10 minutes.

▶ Fill the tortillas with the beef, peppers, and avocado. Serve with the sour cream and the hot sauce, if desired.

TIP
Slice the meat across the grain to break up chewy fibers and make it more tender.

Gouda cheeseburgers with fennel-onion relish

hands-on time: 30 minutes / total time: 30 minutes / serves 4

2 pounds medium sweet potatoes (about 4), peeled and cut into ½-inch wedges

3 tablespoons plus 1 teaspoon olive oil
  Kosher salt and black pepper

½ small fennel bulb, cored and thinly sliced

½ small red onion, thinly sliced

3 tablespoons fresh lemon juice

1¼ pounds ground beef chuck

4 ounces Gouda, sliced

4 hamburger buns
  Arugula, for serving

▶ Heat oven to 450° F. On a rimmed baking sheet, toss the potatoes with 2 tablespoons of the oil, ¾ teaspoon salt, and ¼ teaspoon pepper. Roast, tossing once, until golden brown and tender, 22 to 25 minutes.

▶ Meanwhile, in a medium bowl, toss the fennel and onion with the lemon juice, 1 tablespoon of the remaining oil, and ¼ teaspoon each salt and pepper; set aside.

▶ Form the beef into four ½-inch-thick patties and season with ½ teaspoon salt and ¼ teaspoon pepper. Heat the remaining teaspoon of oil in a large skillet over medium-high heat. Cook the patties to the desired doneness, 3 to 5 minutes per side for medium. During the last minute of cooking, top the burgers with the Gouda and cook, covered.

▶ Place the burgers on the buns with the arugula and fennel-onion relish. Serve with the fries.

TIP
Sweet potatoes have tender, edible skin. If you scrub them well, you don't have to peel them for this recipe.

lamb chops with curried rice and cherries

hands-on time: 25 minutes / total time: 25 minutes / serves 4

1 cup long-grain white rice
1 teaspoon curry powder
1 cup cherries, halved and
   pitted
½ cup torn fresh basil leaves
1 teaspoon olive oil
8 small lamb rib or loin chops
   (¾ inch thick; about
   2 pounds total)
   Kosher salt and black pepper

▶ Cook the rice according to the package directions, adding the curry powder to the water before cooking. Gently fold the cherries and basil into the cooked rice.

▶ Meanwhile, heat the oil in a large skillet over medium-high heat. Season the lamb with ½ teaspoon salt and ¼ teaspoon pepper. In batches, cook the lamb to the desired doneness, 2 to 4 minutes per side for medium-rare, adding more oil to the pan if necessary. Serve with the rice.

TIP
Turn this meal into a salad the next day. Slice the lamb and serve it, along with the rice, over greens drizzled with your favorite vinaigrette.

classic beef stew

hands-on time: 25 minutes / total time: 3 hours, 40 minutes / serves 8

3 tablespoons all-purpose flour
Kosher salt and black pepper
5 pounds beef chuck, cut into 16 large pieces
2 tablespoons olive oil
1 6-ounce can tomato paste
2 stalks celery, cut into 3-inch lengths
1 medium onion, quartered
1 750-milliliter bottle red wine (such as Pinot Noir or Syrah)
2 bay leaves
2 pounds medium carrots, cut into 3-inch pieces
1½ pounds turnips, peeled and quartered
Buttered egg noodles (optional)

▶ Heat oven to 325° F. In a large bowl, combine the flour, 1½ teaspoons salt, and 1 teaspoon pepper. Add the beef and toss to coat.

▶ Heat the oil in a large pot or Dutch oven over medium-high heat. In batches, brown the beef, turning occasionally, 6 to 8 minutes; transfer to a plate.

▶ Add the tomato paste, celery, onion, wine, bay leaves, a quarter of the carrots, and 2 cups water to the pot. Add the beef and bring to a boil. Cover the pot, transfer to oven, and cook for 2 hours.

▶ Remove the cooked vegetables with a slotted spoon and discard. Skim off and discard any fat. Add the turnips and the remaining carrots. Cover the pot, return it to oven, and cook until the meat and vegetables are tender, 45 to 60 minutes.

▶ If the stew is too thin, place the pot on the stove and simmer, uncovered, until thickened, 5 to 10 minutes more. Serve with the noodles, if desired.

TIP
The stew can be refrigerated, covered, for up to 2 days or frozen for up to 3 months.

steak with potato-parsnip mash

hands-on time: 10 minutes / total time: 35 minutes / serves 4

1 pound Yukon gold potatoes (about 2), peeled and cut into 2-inch pieces
½ pound parsnips (about 2 medium), peeled and cut into 1-inch pieces
Kosher salt and black pepper
½ cup whole milk
2 tablespoons unsalted butter
2 scallions, thinly sliced
1 tablespoon olive oil
1½ pounds sirloin steak (1 inch thick)

▶ Place the potatoes and parsnips in a large pot and add enough cold water to cover. Bring to a boil and add 2 teaspoons salt. Reduce heat and simmer until tender, 15 to 18 minutes; drain and return to the pot. Add the milk, butter, ½ teaspoon salt, and ¼ teaspoon pepper and mash to the desired consistency. Sprinkle with the scallions.

▶ Meanwhile, heat the oil in a large skillet over medium-high heat. Season the steak with ½ teaspoon each salt and pepper and cook to the desired doneness, 4 to 6 minutes per side for medium-rare. Let rest for at least 5 minutes before slicing. Serve with the potato-parsnip mash.

TIP
Resist the temptation to start the potatoes in boiling water. Starting them in cold water brings their temperature up gradually, cooking them more evenly, so they don't end up mushy on the outside and hard in the center.

broccoli rabe and beef flat bread

hands-on time: 15 minutes / total time: 40 minutes / serves 4

1 tablespoon olive oil
½ pound ground beef
1 pound pizza dough, thawed
   if frozen
   Cornmeal, for the pan
1 bunch broccoli rabe,
   chopped (about 2 cups)
½ red onion, sliced
8 ounces mozzarella, grated
   (2 cups)
   Kosher salt and black pepper

▶ Heat oven to 425° F. Heat the oil in a large skillet over medium-high heat. Add the beef and cook, breaking it up with a spoon, until no longer pink, 3 to 4 minutes.

▶ Meanwhile, shape the dough into a large oval and place on a cornmeal-dusted rimmed baking sheet.

▶ Top the dough with the beef, broccoli rabe, onion, and mozzarella and season with ¼ teaspoon each salt and pepper. Bake until golden brown, 20 to 25 minutes.

TIP
Use packaged mozzarella with this recipe. The fresh variety is too moist and will make the dough soggy.

slow-cooker Cuban braised beef and peppers

hands-on time: 10 minutes / total time: 4½ to 8½ hours / serves 4

1   28-ounce can diced
    tomatoes, drained
2   red bell peppers, sliced
    ½ inch thick
1   onion, cut into 8 wedges
2   teaspoons dried oregano
1   teaspoon ground cumin
    Kosher salt and black pepper
1½ pounds flank steak, cut
    crosswise into 3 pieces
1   cup long-grain white rice
1   avocado, sliced
¼   cup fresh cilantro leaves

▶ In a 5- to 6-quart slow cooker, combine the tomatoes, bell peppers, onion, oregano, cumin, 1½ teaspoons salt, and ¼ teaspoon black pepper.

▶ Nestle the beef in the vegetables and cook, covered, until it is tender and pulls apart easily, on high for 4 to 5 hours or on low for 7 to 8 hours.

▶ Twenty-five minutes before serving, cook the rice according to the package directions.

▶ Using 2 forks, shred the beef and fold it into the cooking liquid. Serve with the rice and top with the avocado and cilantro.

TIP
This stew is a take on the Cuban dish ropa vieja. The name means "old clothes" in Spanish, as the strips of meat and colorful vegetables are said to resemble a jumble of rags. Flank steak is traditional, but you can use beef chuck.

grilled steak, plums, and bok choy

hands-on time: 20 minutes / total time: 40 minutes / serves 4

1½ pounds flank steak
¼ cup low-sodium soy sauce
4 plums, cut into wedges
4 heads baby bok choy, halved
   lengthwise
1 tablespoon canola oil
   Kosher salt and black pepper
2 teaspoons toasted sesame
   seeds

▶ Place the steak and soy sauce in a shallow dish and toss to coat. Let the steak marinate, turning occasionally, for at least 15 minutes.

▶ Meanwhile, heat grill to medium-high. In a large bowl, toss the plums and bok choy with the oil, ½ teaspoon salt, and ¼ teaspoon pepper.

▶ Grill the steak to the desired doneness, 4 to 6 minutes per side for medium-rare. Let rest for at least 5 minutes before slicing.

▶ Meanwhile, grill the plums and bok choy until tender, about 2 minutes per side. Serve with the steak and sprinkle with the sesame seeds.

TIP
To enhance the sesame flavor, drizzle the bok choy and plums with a little toasted sesame oil just before serving.

spiced lamb chops with chickpea and carrot sauté

hands-on time: 25 minutes / total time: 25 minutes / serves 4

1 tablespoon plus 1 teaspoon
   olive oil
8 small lamb chops (about
   2 pounds total)
1 teaspoon curry powder
   Kosher salt and black pepper
2 medium carrots, thinly sliced
2 cloves garlic, thinly sliced
1 15.5-ounce can chickpeas,
   rinsed
2 tablespoons fresh lemon juice
2 tablespoons chopped
   fresh dill

▶ Heat oven to 400° F. Heat 1 teaspoon of the oil in a large skillet over medium-high heat. Season the lamb with the curry powder, ¾ teaspoon salt, and ½ teaspoon pepper and cook until browned, 2 to 3 minutes per side. Transfer to a rimmed baking sheet and roast to the desired doneness, 4 to 6 minutes for medium-rare.

▶ Meanwhile, wipe out the skillet and heat the remaining tablespoon of oil over medium-high heat. Add the carrots and cook, tossing frequently, until tender, 6 to 10 minutes.

▶ Add the garlic to the skillet and cook for 1 minute. Add the chickpeas, ½ teaspoon salt, and ¼ teaspoon pepper and cook, tossing occasionally, until heated through, 2 to 3 minutes. Stir in the lemon juice and dill. Serve with the lamb.

TIP
For an even heartier meal, serve this dish with basmati rice tossed with cashews.

beef and sweet potato turnovers

hands-on time: 15 minutes / total time: 45 minutes / serves 4

1 tablespoon olive oil
½ pound ground beef
2 cloves garlic, chopped
1 sweet potato, grated
2 cups baby spinach
  Kosher salt and black pepper
2 sheets frozen puff pastry
  (one 17.3-ounce package),
  thawed
2 ounces Cheddar, grated
  (½ cup)

▶ Heat oven to 400° F. Heat the oil in a large skillet over medium-high heat. Add the beef and cook, breaking it up with a spoon, until no longer pink, 3 to 4 minutes. Stir in the garlic. Remove from heat.

▶ Add the sweet potato, spinach, ½ teaspoon salt, and ¼ teaspoon pepper and toss to combine.

▶ Lay the pastry on a work surface and cut each sheet in half, forming a total of 4 rectangles. Dividing evenly, spoon the beef mixture, then the Cheddar, onto one side of each rectangle, leaving a ¼-inch border.

▶ Fold the dough over the filling and press firmly to seal the edges. Bake on a parchment-lined baking sheet until golden brown, 20 to 25 minutes.

TIP
For nice, shiny crusts, brush the turnovers with a beaten egg yolk before baking.

Cajun skirt steak with creamed corn

hands-on time: 20 minutes / total time: 20 minutes / serves 4

2 tablespoons unsalted butter
1 small onion, chopped
4 cups fresh corn kernels
   (from about 8 ears)
1 cup half-and-half
   Kosher salt and black pepper
1½ pounds skirt steak, cut into
   2 pieces
2 teaspoons blackening or
   Cajun seasoning
4 cups mixed greens
1 cup cherry tomatoes, halved
1 tablespoon olive oil

▶ Melt the butter in a medium saucepan over medium-high heat. Add the onion and cook, stirring occasionally, until beginning to soften, 4 to 5 minutes.

▶ Add the corn, half-and-half, ½ teaspoon salt, and ¼ teaspoon pepper to the saucepan and simmer until the corn is tender and the half-and-half is slightly thickened, 5 to 8 minutes.

▶ Meanwhile, heat broiler. Season the steak with the blackening seasoning and ¼ teaspoon each salt and pepper. Place on a broilerproof rimmed baking sheet and broil to the desired doneness, 3 to 4 minutes per side for medium-rare. Let rest for at least 5 minutes before slicing.

▶ In a medium bowl, toss the greens and tomatoes with the oil and ¼ teaspoon each salt and pepper. Serve with the steak and corn.

TIP
Fresh corn works best in this recipe, but thawed frozen kernels can also be used. To achieve a similar creamy consistency, add 1 tablespoon flour to the softened onions and cook for 1 minute before adding the corn and half-and-half.

spicy beef kebabs with minted watermelon salad
hands-on time: 20 minutes / total time: 20 minutes / serves 4

2 pounds watermelon (about ¼ medium), rind removed, cut into pieces

¼ red onion, thinly sliced

½ cup torn fresh mint leaves
Kosher salt and black pepper

1½ pounds tri-tip or sirloin steak, cut into 1½-inch pieces

8 red jalapeño peppers, sliced into 1-inch-thick rings

1 lime, cut into wedges

▶ Soak 8 wooden skewers for 10 minutes. Heat grill to medium-high.

▶ Meanwhile, arrange the watermelon on a platter. Sprinkle with the onion, mint, and ¼ teaspoon each salt and black pepper; set aside.

▶ Thread the beef and jalapeños onto the skewers and season with ½ teaspoon each salt and black pepper. Grill, turning frequently, to the desired doneness, 6 to 8 minutes for medium-rare.

▶ Serve with the lime wedges and watermelon salad.

TIP
Before buying a precut piece of watermelon, look closely. Cut sides with flesh that appears mealy or is separating from the seeds indicate that the fruit is old.

lamb with golden Israeli couscous

hands-on time: 15 minutes / total time: 25 minutes / serves 4

2 tablespoons olive oil

3 lamb shoulder chops (1 inch thick; about 2 pounds total)

1 teaspoon paprika

½ teaspoon ground cinnamon
   Kosher salt and black pepper

1 medium onion, chopped

1¼ cups Israeli couscous (also labeled "pearl couscous")

½ cup dried apricots, quartered

1 large pinch saffron (optional)

4 cups baby spinach (about 4 ounces)

▶ Heat 1 tablespoon of the oil in a large skillet over medium-high heat. Season the lamb with the paprika, cinnamon, ½ teaspoon salt, and ¼ teaspoon pepper and cook to the desired doneness, 4 to 6 minutes per side for medium-rare. Let rest for at least 5 minutes before slicing.

▶ Meanwhile, heat the remaining tablespoon of oil in a medium saucepan over medium-high heat. Add the onion and cook, stirring occasionally, until softened, 3 to 4 minutes.

▶ Add the couscous, apricots, saffron (if desired), 1 teaspoon salt, ¼ teaspoon pepper, and 2 cups water to the saucepan, stir, and bring to a boil. Reduce heat and gently simmer, covered, until the couscous is tender and the water is absorbed, 8 to 10 minutes. Fold in the spinach and serve with the lamb.

TIP
Israeli couscous looks like a grain but is really a pearl-shaped pasta that is toasted, giving it a slightly nutty flavor. Like conventional couscous, it is delicious served hot or at room temperature. For a cool summer salad, toss it with olive oil, cucumbers, Feta, and mint.

steak with potato salad and blue cheese vinaigrette

hands-on time: 15 minutes / total time: 30 minutes / serves 4

1 pound red new potatoes (about 12)
Kosher salt and black pepper

¼ cup plus 1 tablespoon olive oil

4 small steaks (such as Newport, flat iron, or top round; 1 inch thick; about 1½ pounds total)

1 ounce blue cheese, crumbled (¼ cup)

2 tablespoons white wine vinegar

1 small head Boston lettuce, torn (about 4 cups)

▶ Place the potatoes in a large saucepan and add enough cold water to cover. Bring to a boil and add 2 teaspoons salt. Reduce heat and simmer until tender, 14 to 16 minutes. Drain, run under cold water to cool, and using a fork, break the potatoes in half.

▶ Meanwhile, heat 1 tablespoon of the oil in a large skillet over medium-high heat. Season the steaks with 1 teaspoon salt and ¾ teaspoon pepper and cook to the desired doneness, 4 to 5 minutes per side for medium-rare.

▶ In a large bowl, combine the blue cheese, vinegar, the remaining ¼ cup of oil, ½ teaspoon salt, and ¼ teaspoon pepper. Add the lettuce and potatoes and toss to coat. Serve with the steaks.

TIP
Any type of blue cheese will work with this vinaigrette. Try spicy Maytag Blue, earthy Stilton, creamy Gorgonzola, or salty, strong-flavored Roquefort.

sweet and spicy beef stir-fry

hands-on time: 20 minutes / total time: 20 minutes / serves 4

8 ounces lo mein noodles
1 tablespoon canola oil
1 pound flank steak, thinly
  sliced across the grain
  Kosher salt and black pepper
½ pound snow peas, halved
  lengthwise
2 medium carrots, thinly sliced
2 shallots, sliced
⅓ cup red pepper jelly

▶ Cook the noodles according to the package directions.

▶ Meanwhile, heat the oil in a large skillet over medium-high heat. Season the beef with ½ teaspoon salt and ¼ teaspoon pepper and cook, tossing occasionally, until cooked through, 3 to 4 minutes; transfer to a plate.

▶ Add the snow peas, carrots, and shallots to the skillet and cook, tossing occasionally, for 4 minutes.

▶ Return the beef to the skillet, add the jelly, and cook, tossing, for 1 minute. Serve with the noodles.

TIP
To make the meat easier to slice thinly, firm it up first in the freezer for 10 to 15 minutes.

deep-dish cheeseburger pizza

hands-on time: 15 minutes / total time: 35 minutes / serves 4

1 tablespoon plus 1 teaspoon olive oil, plus more for the skillet

½ pound ground beef

¼ cup barbecue sauce

1 pound pizza dough, thawed if frozen

4 ounces Cheddar, grated (1 cup)

1 cup baby arugula

1 small tomato, sliced

¼ small red onion, thinly sliced

Kosher salt and black pepper

▶ Heat oven to 425° F. Heat 1 teaspoon of the oil in a large skillet over medium-high heat. Add the beef and cook, breaking it up with a spoon, until no longer pink, 4 to 5 minutes. Stir in the barbecue sauce.

▶ Oil a 10-inch ovenproof skillet. Press the dough into the bottom and up the sides. Top the dough with the beef and sprinkle with the Cheddar. Bake until golden brown, 20 to 25 minutes.

▶ Top the pizza with the arugula, tomato, and onion. Drizzle with the remaining tablespoon of oil and sprinkle with a pinch each of salt and pepper.

TIP
If you don't have a 10-inch oven-proof skillet, use a 9-inch cake pan.

Tuscan lamb with garlicky tomato sauce and polenta

hands-on time: 15 minutes / total time: 25 minutes / serves 4

1 teaspoon olive oil

8 small lamb loin chops (¾ inch thick; about 2 pounds total)

Kosher salt and black pepper

2 cloves garlic, sliced

1 28-ounce can diced tomatoes

½ cup dry white wine

1 tablespoon fresh rosemary leaves

¾ cup instant polenta

1 tablespoon unsalted butter

▶ Heat oven to 400° F. Heat the oil in a large ovenproof skillet over medium-high heat. Season the lamb with ½ teaspoon salt and ¼ teaspoon pepper and cook until browned, 2 to 3 minutes per side; transfer to a plate. Spoon off and discard all but 1 tablespoon of the drippings.

▶ Add the garlic to the skillet and cook, stirring, until fragrant, 30 seconds. Add the tomatoes, wine, rosemary, and ¼ teaspoon each salt and pepper and bring to a boil. Reduce heat and simmer until the sauce begins to thicken, 2 to 3 minutes.

▶ Nestle the lamb in the tomatoes. Transfer the skillet to oven and cook to the desired doneness, 10 to 12 minutes for medium-rare.

▶ Meanwhile, in a medium saucepan, bring 3 cups water to a boil. Gradually whisk in the polenta. Cook, whisking frequently, until thickened, 3 to 4 minutes. Whisk in the butter, ½ teaspoon salt, and ⅛ teaspoon pepper. Serve with the lamb and tomato sauce.

TIP
In a pinch, you can substitute finely ground cornmeal for instant polenta. Cook according to the package directions for cornmeal mush.

steak sandwiches with Brie

hands-on time: 15 minutes / total time: 15 minutes / serves 4

1 tablespoon olive oil
½ pound flank steak
   Kosher salt and black pepper
1 baguette
1 cup baby arugula
8 ounces Brie, sliced
¼ small red onion, sliced

▶ Heat the oil in a large skillet over medium-high heat. Season the steak with ½ teaspoon salt and ¼ teaspoon pepper and cook to the desired doneness, 4 to 5 minutes per side for medium-rare. Let rest for at least 5 minutes before slicing.

▶ Split the baguette horizontally, then cut it crosswise into 4 pieces. Form sandwiches with the bread, arugula, steak, Brie, and onion.

TIP
For a bit of sharpness, spread the bread with Dijon mustard. Or try a dollop of fruit chutney to play off the creaminess of the cheese.

steak with crispy potatoes and pistachio pesto

hands-on time: 30 minutes / total time: 35 minutes / serves 4

1½ pounds red new potatoes
(about 18), sliced ¼ inch thick

¼ cup plus 3 tablespoons
olive oil

Kosher salt and black pepper

½ cup fresh flat-leaf parsley
leaves

¼ cup shelled roasted pistachios

1 small clove garlic

2 strip or sirloin steaks (1 inch
thick; about 1½ pounds total)

1 bunch broccoli rabe (about
1 pound)

▶ Heat oven to 425° F. On a large rimmed baking sheet, toss the potatoes with 2 tablespoons of the oil and ¼ teaspoon each salt and pepper. Roast until golden, 25 to 30 minutes.

▶ Meanwhile, in a food processor, process the parsley, pistachios, garlic, ¼ cup of the remaining oil, and ¼ teaspoon each salt and pepper until finely chopped.

▶ Heat the remaining tablespoon of oil in a large skillet over medium-high heat. Season the steaks with ½ teaspoon each salt and pepper and cook to the desired doneness, 4 to 6 minutes per side for medium-rare. Transfer to a cutting board and let rest for at least 5 minutes before slicing.

▶ Wipe out the skillet. Add the broccoli rabe and ½ cup water and simmer, covered, until tender, 2 to 3 minutes. Serve with the steak, potatoes, and pesto.

TIP
The pistachio pesto in this dish makes an excellent accompaniment to lamb, chicken, shrimp, or fish. Or serve it on toasted country bread for an easy appetizer.

balsamic-glazed lamb meat loaf

hands-on time: 25 minutes / total time: 50 minutes / serves 4

2 slices white sandwich bread, torn into small pieces
1 pound ground lamb
1 large egg
4 cloves garlic, chopped
2 tablespoons fresh thyme leaves
    Kosher salt and black pepper
2 tablespoons balsamic vinegar
2 tablespoons olive oil
1 small red bell pepper, thinly sliced
½ red onion, thinly sliced
2 15.5-ounce cans cannellini beans, rinsed
1 tablespoon fresh lemon juice

▶ Heat oven to 400° F. In a large bowl, combine the bread and 3 tablespoons water. Add the lamb, egg, half the garlic, 1 tablespoon of the thyme, ¾ teaspoon salt, and ¼ teaspoon black pepper and toss gently to combine.

▶ Place the mixture on a foil-lined rimmed baking sheet and shape into a 6-inch-long loaf (about 3 inches thick). Bake, brushing with the vinegar several times during cooking, until a thermometer inserted in the center registers 160° F, 30 to 35 minutes. Let rest for at least 5 minutes before slicing.

▶ Meanwhile, heat the oil in a large skillet over medium heat. Add the bell pepper, onion, and the remaining garlic and thyme and cook, tossing occasionally, until the vegetables begin to soften, 4 to 5 minutes. Add the beans, ½ teaspoon salt, and ¼ teaspoon black pepper and cook until heated through, 2 to 3 minutes more. Stir in the lemon juice. Serve with the meat loaf.

TIP
Short on time? Form the lamb mixture into 4 patties and cook in olive oil in a large skillet over medium-high heat, 3 to 5 minutes per side.

cottage pies

hands-on time: 20 minutes / total time: 40 minutes / serves 4

1½ pounds Yukon gold potatoes (about 3), peeled and cut into 2-inch pieces
Kosher salt and black pepper
½ cup whole milk
2 tablespoons unsalted butter
1 tablespoon olive oil
1 pound ground beef
⅓ cup ketchup
1 tablespoon Worcestershire sauce
1½ cups frozen peas and carrots

▶ Heat oven to 425° F. Place the potatoes in a large pot and add enough cold water to cover. Bring to a boil and add 2 teaspoons salt. Reduce heat and simmer until just tender, 15 to 18 minutes. Drain the potatoes and return them to the pot. Add the milk, butter, and ¼ teaspoon each salt and pepper and mash to the desired consistency.

▶ Meanwhile, heat the oil in a large skillet over medium-high heat. Add the beef and cook, breaking it up with a spoon, until no longer pink, 5 to 6 minutes. Stir in the ketchup, Worcestershire sauce, ½ teaspoon salt, and ¼ teaspoon pepper. Fold in the peas and carrots.

▶ Transfer the beef mixture to 4 individual baking dishes and top with the mashed potatoes. Bake until golden brown, 15 to 20 minutes.

TIP
The pies can be assembled (but not baked) up to 2 days in advance; refrigerate, covered. Bake straight from the refrigerator, adding 10 minutes to the baking time.

quick beef tacos

hands-on time: 20 minutes / total time: 20 minutes / serves 4

1½ pounds ground beef
1½ cups jarred salsa
 1 teaspoon ground cumin
    Kosher salt
 8 taco shells
 1 avocado, diced
½ cup sour cream
½ cup fresh cilantro sprigs

▶ Heat a large skillet over medium-high heat. Add the beef and cook, breaking it up with a spoon, until browned, 6 to 8 minutes. Spoon off and discard any drippings.

▶ Add 1 cup of the salsa, the cumin, and ¾ teaspoon salt to the skillet and cook, stirring occasionally, until heated through, 2 to 3 minutes.

▶ Dividing evenly, fill the taco shells with the beef mixture and top with the avocado, sour cream, cilantro, and the remaining ½ cup of salsa.

TIP
Give this dish a healthy upgrade by substituting ground turkey for the beef.

slow-cooker corned beef, Brussels sprouts, and carrots

hands-on time: 15 minutes / total time: 4 to 8 hours / serves 4 (with leftovers)

1 pound carrots, cut into
   3-inch pieces

1 12-ounce bottle amber ale

1 3-pound piece corned beef
   brisket (with spice packet,
   if included)

¾ pound Brussels sprouts

½ cup sour cream

2 tablespoons whole-grain
   mustard

1 tablespoon chopped fresh
   tarragon

▶ In a 5- to 6-quart slow cooker, combine the carrots, amber ale, and contents of the spice packet (if included). Nestle the beef in the carrots and cook, covered, until tender, on high for 4 to 5 hours or on low for 7 to 8 hours.

▶ Ten minutes before serving, thinly slice the Brussels sprouts. (This is easiest to do in a food processor fitted with the slicing blade.)

▶ Transfer the beef to a cutting board. If the slow cooker is on the low setting, turn it to high. Add the Brussels sprouts to the carrots in the slow cooker and cook, covered, until the Brussels sprouts are tender, 4 to 6 minutes.

▶ Meanwhile, in a small bowl, combine the sour cream, mustard, and tarragon.

▶ Slice the beef and serve with the vegetables and sour cream sauce.

TIP
Corned beef brisket sold in the super-market meat case is uncooked, unlike the cooked corned beef at the deli counter. Brisket that comes without a packet of spices has already been cured.

seared lamb chops with minted spaghetti squash

hands-on time: 15 minutes / total time: 30 minutes / serves 4

1 small spaghetti squash
  (about 3 pounds)
3 tablespoons olive oil
4 small lamb shoulder chops
  (1 inch thick; about 2½
  pounds total)
½ teaspoon ground cumin
  Kosher salt and black pepper
4 scallions, thinly sliced
¼ cup fresh mint, sliced

▶ Cut ½ inch from each end of the squash, then cut the squash in half lengthwise. Microwave on a plate, cut-side down, on high until tender, 10 to 12 minutes. Let cool for 5 minutes.

▶ Meanwhile, heat 1 tablespoon of the oil in a large skillet over medium-high heat. Season the lamb with the cumin, ½ teaspoon salt, and ¼ teaspoon pepper. Cook to the desired doneness, 4 to 5 minutes per side for medium-rare.

▶ Scoop out and discard the squash seeds. With a fork, gently scrape the strands of squash flesh into a large bowl. Toss with the scallions, mint, the remaining 2 tablespoons of oil, ½ teaspoon salt, and ¼ teaspoon pepper. Serve with the lamb.

TIP
Fresh herbs add zest to exceedingly mild spaghetti squash. If you don't have mint, try parsley, basil, tarragon, or chives.

dinner tonight:
pork

roasted pork chops and peaches

hands-on time: 20 minutes / total time: 30 minutes / serves 4

1 10-ounce package couscous
   (1½ cups)
1 tablespoon olive oil
4 bone-in pork chops (¾ inch
   thick; about 2 pounds total)
   Kosher salt and black pepper
2 peaches, cut into wedges
1 small red onion, cut into thin
   wedges
3 tablespoons white wine
   vinegar
½ cup fresh basil leaves

▶ Heat oven to 400° F. Cook the couscous according to the package directions.

▶ Meanwhile, heat the oil in a large ovenproof skillet over medium-high heat. Season the pork with ½ teaspoon salt and ¼ teaspoon pepper and cook until browned, 3 to 5 minutes per side. Transfer to a plate.

▶ Add the peaches, onion, vinegar, and ¼ teaspoon each salt and pepper to the skillet and cook, tossing, for 1 minute. Return the pork and any accumulated juices to the skillet.

▶ Transfer the skillet to oven and roast until the pork is cooked through and the peaches are tender, 8 to 10 minutes. Serve with the couscous and sprinkle with the basil.

TIP
Nectarines or plums also work nicely in this recipe.

brown sugar–glazed pork with grilled corn

hands-on time: 15 minutes / total time: 35 minutes / serves 4

¼ cup Worcestershire sauce
2 tablespoons brown sugar
1 pork tenderloin (about
   1¼ pounds)
   Kosher salt and black pepper
4 ears corn, shucked
2 tablespoons unsalted butter
2 scallions, sliced

▶ Heat grill to medium-high. In a small bowl, mix together the Worcestershire sauce and brown sugar.

▶ Season the pork with ½ teaspoon salt and ¼ teaspoon pepper. Grill, turning often, until the internal temperature registers 145° F, 20 to 25 minutes, brushing with the brown sugar glaze during the last 5 minutes of cooking. Let rest for at least 5 minutes before slicing.

▶ Meanwhile, grill the corn, turning occasionally, until tender and slightly charred, 6 to 8 minutes. Cut the kernels off the cobs into a medium bowl and toss with the butter, scallions, ½ teaspoon salt, and ¼ teaspoon pepper. Serve with the pork.

TIP
When cutting corn off the cob, stand the cob on end in a wide, shallow bowl or on a rimmed baking sheet to catch the kernels and juices.

sausage and white bean casserole

hands-on time: 15 minutes / total time: 45 minutes / serves 4

- 1 tablespoon plus 1 teaspoon olive oil
- 1 pound Italian sausage links (about 8)
- 2 carrots, cut into ½-inch pieces
- 2 cloves garlic, chopped
- 2 bunches Swiss chard, thick stems removed and leaves cut into 2-inch strips (about 12 cups)
- 2 15.5-ounce cans cannellini beans, rinsed
  Kosher salt and black pepper
- 2 tablespoons bread crumbs

▶ Heat oven to 400° F. Heat 1 tablespoon of the oil in a large ovenproof skillet over medium-high heat. Add the sausages and cook, turning occasionally, until browned, 5 to 6 minutes. Transfer to a plate.

▶ Add the carrots and garlic to the skillet and cook, stirring frequently, for 1 minute. Add the chard and cook until wilted, 1 to 2 minutes more.

▶ Add the beans, ½ cup water, and ¼ teaspoon each salt and pepper to the skillet. Nestle the sausages in the beans and bring to a boil.

▶ In a small bowl, combine the bread crumbs and the remaining teaspoon of oil. Sprinkle over the sausage mixture. Transfer the skillet to oven and bake until golden, 25 to 30 minutes.

TIP
Play up the earthy flavors of this hearty casserole by using parsnips or turnips in place of— or in addition to— the carrots.

paprika-spiced pork chops with spinach sauté

hands-on time: 20 minutes / total time: 25 minutes / serves 4

1 tablespoon olive oil

4 bone-in pork chops (1 inch thick; about 2½ pounds total)

1 teaspoon paprika
Kosher salt and black pepper

4 scallions, sliced

¼ cup golden raisins

1 10-ounce package spinach, thick stems removed (about 16 loosely packed cups)

1 tablespoon fresh lemon juice

▶ Heat oven to 400° F. Heat the oil in a large skillet over medium-high heat. Season the pork with the paprika, ½ teaspoon salt, and ¼ teaspoon pepper and cook until browned, 2 to 3 minutes per side.

▶ Transfer the pork to a rimmed baking sheet and roast until cooked through, 10 to 12 minutes.

▶ Meanwhile, return the skillet to medium heat, add the scallions and raisins, and cook, stirring, for 30 seconds. Add the spinach and ¼ teaspoon each salt and pepper and cook, tossing, until just wilted, 1 to 2 minutes more. Stir in the lemon juice. Serve with the pork.

TIP
To add a touch of smoky flavor, substitute smoked paprika (often labeled "pimentón") for the usual sweet variety.

ham, Gruyère, and shallot pizza

hands-on time: 15 minutes / total time: 50 minutes / serves 6

1 pound pizza dough, thawed
  if frozen
  Cornmeal, for the pan

2 tablespoons olive oil

2 shallots, sliced into thin rings

12 sprigs fresh thyme
  Kosher salt and black pepper

½ pound thinly sliced cooked
  ham

2 ounces Gruyère or Swiss
  cheese, grated (½ cup)

▶ Heat oven to 425° F. Shape the dough into a 14-inch round and place on a cornmeal-dusted rimmed baking sheet.

▶ Brush the dough with 1 tablespoon of the oil and bake until puffed and golden, 15 to 20 minutes.

▶ Meanwhile, in a medium bowl, toss the shallots and thyme with the remaining tablespoon of oil and ¼ teaspoon each salt and pepper.

▶ Top the partially cooked dough with the ham, shallot mixture, and Gruyère. Bake until the crust is crisp and the cheese has melted, 12 to 15 minutes.

TIP
To thaw frozen pizza dough quickly, place it in a resealable plastic bag and set it in a bowl of cold water for 10 to 20 minutes.

pork chops with garlicky broccoli

hands-on time: 20 minutes / total time: 20 minutes / serves 4

1 cup long-grain white rice

3 tablespoons olive oil

4 bone-in pork chops (1 inch
  thick; about 2½ pounds total)
  Kosher salt and black pepper

1 bunch broccoli, cut into
  florets

2 cloves garlic, chopped

2 tablespoons low-sodium
  soy sauce

▶ Heat oven to 400° F. Cook the rice according to the package directions.

▶ Meanwhile, heat 1 tablespoon of the oil in a large ovenproof skillet over medium-high heat. Season the pork with ½ teaspoon salt and ¼ teaspoon pepper and cook until browned, 2 to 3 minutes per side. Transfer the skillet to oven and roast the pork until cooked through, 6 to 8 minutes.

▶ Meanwhile, heat the remaining 2 tablespoons of oil in a second large skillet over medium-high heat. Add the broccoli, garlic, soy sauce, and ⅓ cup water. Cook, covered, until the broccoli is tender, 5 to 6 minutes. Serve with the pork and rice.

TIP
For fluffier rice, before cooking, rinse the grains in a sieve under cold water until the water runs clear.

jalapeño pork stew with pickled onions

hands-on time: 30 minutes / total time: 3 hours, 45 minutes / serves 8

 4 tablespoons olive oil
 5 pounds boneless pork
   shoulder or butt, trimmed
   and cut into 2-inch pieces
 2 teaspoons ground cumin
   Kosher salt and black pepper
 3 tablespoons all-purpose flour
 1 cup fresh orange juice
 1 14.5-ounce can diced
   tomatoes, drained
12 cloves garlic
 1 to 2 jalapeño peppers,
   seeded and sliced
 1 large red onion, thinly sliced
¼ cup red wine vinegar
 1 1-pound package frozen
   cut okra
1½ cups grits

▶ Heat oven to 325° F. Heat 2 tablespoons of the oil in a large ovenproof pot or Dutch oven over medium-high heat. Season the pork with the cumin, 1½ teaspoons salt, and ½ teaspoon black pepper. In batches, cook the pork until browned, turning occasionally, 6 to 8 minutes; transfer to a plate.

▶ Add the flour and the remaining 2 tablespoons of oil to the pot and cook, stirring, for 1 minute. Add the orange juice, tomatoes, garlic, jalapeños, and 4 cups water and bring to a boil. Return the pork to the pot, cover, transfer to oven, and cook until the pork is tender, 2½ to 3 hours.

▶ Meanwhile, in a small bowl, toss the onion with the vinegar, ½ cup water, and ½ teaspoon salt. Let sit, tossing occasionally, for at least 30 minutes (and up to 4 hours).

▶ Skim off and discard any fat from the stew. Add the okra. Cover the pot, return it to oven, and cook until the okra is tender, about 15 minutes. If the stew is too thin, place the pot on the stove and simmer, uncovered, until thickened, 5 to 10 minutes more.

▶ Meanwhile, cook the grits according to the package directions. Serve with the stew and marinated onions.

TIP
Seeding the jalapeños removes a good deal of their heat while retaining their distinctive flavor.

apricot-glazed ham with potatoes and asparagus

hands-on time: 15 minutes / total time: 1 hour / serves 4 (with leftover ham)

1   3-pound boneless ham
¼   cup apricot preserves
1   pound fingerling or some
    other small potatoes
    (about 12)
    Kosher salt and black pepper
1   pound asparagus, cut into
    1-inch pieces
3   tablespoons olive oil
1   tablespoon white wine
    vinegar
1   tablespoon prepared
    horseradish
¼   cup fresh dill sprigs

▶ Heat oven to 350° F. Place the ham on a foil-lined rimmed baking sheet and cook until heated through, 50 to 60 minutes, spreading the ham with the preserves after 20 minutes of cooking.

▶ Meanwhile, place the potatoes in a large saucepan and add enough cold water to cover. Bring to a boil and add 1 teaspoon salt. Reduce heat and simmer until tender, 15 to 18 minutes.

▶ With a slotted spoon, transfer the potatoes to a colander. Run under cold water to cool, then cut into quarters.

▶ Return the water in the saucepan to a boil. Add the asparagus and cook until tender, 2 to 3 minutes. Drain and run under cold water to cool.

▶ In a large bowl, whisk together the oil, vinegar, horseradish, ½ teaspoon salt, and ¼ teaspoon pepper. Add the potatoes and asparagus and toss to combine; fold in the dill. Thinly slice the ham and serve with the vegetables.

TIP
To keep leftover ham from drying out, slice only what you will use for dinner and wrap the rest. The ham will last for up to 4 days in the refrigerator. Reheat, if desired, and slice just before serving.

spiced pork chops with red cabbage

hands-on time: 25 minutes / total time: 25 minutes / serves 4

3 tablespoons olive oil
4 bone-in pork chops
  (1 inch thick; about 2½
  pounds total)
1 teaspoon ground cumin
  Kosher salt and black pepper
1 onion, sliced
½ small head red cabbage,
  thinly sliced (about 6 cups)
½ cup golden raisins
¼ cup red wine vinegar
¼ cup chopped fresh dill
  Country bread (optional)

▶ Heat 1 tablespoon of the oil in a large skillet over medium heat. Season the pork with the cumin, ½ teaspoon salt, and ¼ teaspoon pepper and cook until browned and cooked through, 6 to 8 minutes per side.

▶ Meanwhile, heat the remaining 2 tablespoons of oil in a second large skillet over medium-high heat. Cook the onion, stirring occasionally, until softened, 3 to 4 minutes.

▶ Add the cabbage, raisins, vinegar, ¼ cup water, ¾ teaspoon salt, and ¼ teaspoon pepper to the onion. Cook, covered, tossing occasionally, until just tender, 6 to 8 minutes more; fold in the dill. Serve with the pork and the bread, if desired.

TIP
Turn leftovers into sandwiches the next day: Slice the meat and layer it with the cabbage on rye bread or kaiser rolls spread with mustard.

sausage and broccoli calzones

hands-on time: 15 minutes / total time: 45 minutes / serves 4

1 teaspoon olive oil, plus more
   for baking sheet and dough
1 pound Italian sausage links
   (about 8)
1 pound pizza dough, thawed if
   frozen
12 ounces mozzarella, grated
   (3 cups)
2 cups chopped broccoli
1 cup marinara sauce

▶ Heat oven to 425° F. Brush a large rimmed baking sheet with oil.

▶ Heat the oil in a large skillet over medium-high heat. Cook the sausages, turning occasionally, until browned and cooked through, 10 to 12 minutes; slice.

▶ Shape the dough into four 8-inch rounds. Dividing evenly, top half of each round with the sausages, mozzarella, and broccoli. Fold the dough over and pinch the edges to seal.

▶ Place the calzones on the prepared baking sheet and brush with oil. Bake until golden brown, 25 to 30 minutes. Serve with the marinara sauce.

TIP
These calzones are a great make-ahead meal. Freeze them (unbaked) on a parchment-lined baking sheet just until firm, 15 to 20 minutes, then transfer to freezer-safe resealable bags and freeze for up to 3 months. Bake them from frozen on a parchment-lined baking sheet, adding 10 minutes to the baking time.

meatballs with pine nuts and raisins

hands-on time: 25 minutes / total time: 25 minutes / serves 4

1¼ pounds ground pork
¼ cup pine nuts
¼ cup chopped raisins or
currants
¼ teaspoon ground cinnamon
Kosher salt and black pepper
1 tablespoon olive oil
2 cloves garlic, thinly sliced
2 bunches Swiss chard, thick
stems removed and leaves
cut into 2-inch strips (about
12 cups)
1 small baguette, sliced

▶ Heat broiler. In a large bowl, combine the pork, pine nuts, raisins, cinnamon, 1 teaspoon salt, and ¼ teaspoon pepper.

▶ Form the pork mixture into 20 walnut-size meatballs and place on a foil-lined rimmed baking sheet. Broil, turning once, until cooked through, 6 to 8 minutes.

▶ Meanwhile, heat the oil in a large saucepan over medium heat. Add the garlic and cook, stirring, until golden, 1 to 2 minutes. Add the chard, ½ teaspoon salt, and ¼ teaspoon pepper and cook, tossing occasionally, until wilted, 3 to 4 minutes more. Serve with the meatballs and bread.

TIP
Shaping meatballs can be sticky business. Wet your hands with cold water first (and repeat as needed) to keep things clean.

pork chops with mustard sauce and tarragon

hands-on time: 15 minutes / total time: 20 minutes / serves 4

3 tablespoons olive oil
4 boneless pork chops (1 inch thick; about 1½ pounds total)
Kosher salt and black pepper
2 shallots, finely chopped
¾ cup dry white wine
2 tablespoons heavy cream
1 tablespoon Dijon mustard
1 small head frisée, torn into pieces (about 4 cups)
1 lemon, cut into wedges
1 tablespoon chopped fresh tarragon

▶ Heat oven to 400° F. Heat 1 tablespoon of the oil in a large skillet over medium-high heat. Season the pork with ½ teaspoon each salt and pepper and cook until browned, 2 to 3 minutes per side. Transfer to a rimmed baking sheet and roast until cooked through, 5 to 7 minutes.

▶ Meanwhile, add the shallots and 1 tablespoon of the remaining oil to the skillet and cook, stirring frequently, until soft, 3 to 4 minutes. Add the wine and simmer until reduced by half, 1 to 2 minutes. Add the cream and simmer until the sauce just thickens, about 1 minute more. Whisk in the mustard.

▶ In a large bowl, toss the frisée with the remaining tablespoon of oil. Serve with the pork, sauce, and lemon wedges. Sprinkle the pork with the tarragon.

TIP
If you don't have heavy cream, sour cream will work. After simmering the wine and shallots, remove the skillet from the heat and whisk in the mustard and 2 tablespoons sour cream.

tapas plate with marinated chickpeas

hands-on time: 15 minutes / total time: 15 minutes / serves 4

1 15.5-ounce can chickpeas, rinsed
½ cup raisins
¼ cup chopped roasted red peppers
¼ cup chopped fresh flat-leaf parsley
2 scallions, sliced
3 tablespoons olive oil
Kosher salt and black pepper
½ pound manchego, sliced
¼ pound thinly sliced Serrano ham or prosciutto
½ cup mixed olives
½ small loaf country bread

▶ In a medium bowl, toss the chickpeas, raisins, roasted red peppers, parsley, and scallions with the oil, ½ teaspoon salt, and ¼ teaspoon black pepper.

▶ Serve with the manchego, ham, olives, and bread.

TIP
This chickpea mixture is also delicious served over greens for a hearty main-course salad.

grilled pork chops and cherry tomatoes

hands-on time: 20 minutes / total time: 25 minutes / serves 4

- 4 tablespoons (½ stick) unsalted butter, at room temperature
- 1 clove garlic, finely chopped
- 1 teaspoon fresh thyme leaves
- 4 bone-in pork chops (1 inch thick; about 2½ pounds total) Kosher salt and black pepper
- 2 pounds cherry tomatoes

▶ Heat grill to medium-high. In a small bowl, combine the butter, garlic, and thyme; set aside.

▶ Season the pork with ½ teaspoon each salt and pepper and grill until cooked through, 6 to 7 minutes per side.

▶ Meanwhile, divide the tomatoes between 2 pieces of heavy-duty foil and season with ½ teaspoon salt and ¼ teaspoon pepper. Fold the foil over and seal to form 2 pouches. Grill the pouches alongside the pork, gently shaking occasionally, until the tomatoes have softened, 7 to 8 minutes.

▶ Top the pork chops with the garlic butter and serve with the tomatoes.

TIP
Almost any type of fresh herb will work in this recipe. If you don't have thyme, try oregano, marjoram, chives, or tarragon.

roasted pork with Brussels sprouts and apricots

hands-on time: 20 minutes / total time: 25 minutes / serves 4

2 tablespoons olive oil
1 pork tenderloin (about
   1¼ pounds)
   Kosher salt and black pepper
12 ounces Brussels sprouts,
   thinly sliced
¼ cup dried apricots, chopped
2 tablespoons unsalted
   roasted almonds, chopped

▶ Heat oven to 400° F. Heat 1 tablespoon of the oil in a large ovenproof skillet over medium-high heat. Season the pork with ½ teaspoon salt and ¼ teaspoon pepper and cook, turning occasionally, until browned, 6 to 8 minutes.

▶ Transfer the skillet to oven and roast the pork until the internal temperature registers 145° F, 10 to 12 minutes. Let rest for at least 5 minutes before slicing.

▶ Meanwhile, heat the remaining tablespoon of oil in a second large skillet over medium-high heat. Add the Brussels sprouts, apricots, almonds, ½ teaspoon salt, and ¼ teaspoon pepper and cook, tossing occasionally, until the Brussels sprouts are just tender, 3 to 4 minutes. Serve with the pork.

TIP
These sautéed Brussels sprouts are also delicious served with steak or chicken.

201

pork chops with butter bean salad

hands-on time: 20 minutes / total time: 30 minutes / serves 4

1 slice sandwich bread, torn
   into pieces
4 tablespoons olive oil
2 scallions, sliced
   Kosher salt and black pepper
4 boneless pork chops (1 inch
   thick; about 1½ pounds total)
1 bunch spinach, thick stems
   removed and leaves thinly
   sliced (about 4 cups)
1 14-ounce can butter beans,
   rinsed
1 tablespoon red wine vinegar
½ teaspoon dried oregano

▶ Heat oven to 400° F. In a food processor, pulse the bread and 2 tablespoons of the oil to form coarse crumbs. Spread on a rimmed baking sheet and bake until crisp, 5 to 6 minutes. Toss with the scallions, ½ teaspoon salt, and ⅛ teaspoon pepper.

▶ Meanwhile, heat 1 tablespoon of the remaining oil in a large ovenproof skillet over medium-high heat. Season the pork with ½ teaspoon each salt and pepper and cook until browned, 2 to 3 minutes per side. Transfer the skillet to oven and roast the pork until cooked through, 6 to 8 minutes.

▶ In a large bowl, toss the spinach and beans with the vinegar, oregano, the remaining tablespoon of oil, ½ teaspoon salt, and ⅛ teaspoon pepper. Top the pork with the bread crumb mixture. Serve with the salad.

TIP
In a rush? To toast the bread crumbs quickly, spread them on a microwave-safe plate (no oil needed) and cook on high (power level 10) in 1-minute intervals, tossing in between, until golden, 2 to 3 minutes total.

gingery pork and cucumber pitas

hands-on time: 15 minutes / total time: 15 minutes / serves 4

¼ cup rice vinegar
2 teaspoons sugar
  Kosher salt
2 Kirby cucumbers, thinly sliced
1 red or green jalapeño pepper, thinly sliced and seeded, if desired, for less heat
1 tablespoon olive oil
1 pound ground pork
¼ cup hoisin sauce
1 tablespoon grated fresh ginger
4 pitas, halved

▶ In a medium bowl, combine the vinegar, sugar, and ¼ teaspoon salt; stir until the sugar dissolves. Add the cucumbers and jalapeño and let sit, tossing occasionally, for at least 5 minutes.

▶ Meanwhile, heat the oil in a large skillet over medium-high heat. Cook the pork, breaking it up with a spoon, until no longer pink, 5 to 6 minutes. Stir in the hoisin, ginger, and 2 tablespoons water.

▶ Dividing evenly, fill the pita halves with the pork and the cucumber salad.

TIP
Try this refreshing cucumber salad in a ham sandwich or as a burger topping.

cranberry-stuffed pork chops with roasted carrots

hands-on time: 15 minutes / total time: 35 minutes / serves 4

1½ pounds carrots, thinly sliced
1 small red onion, sliced
3 tablespoons olive oil
Kosher salt and black pepper
½ cup dried cranberries, chopped
2 tablespoons apricot preserves
½ teaspoon ground coriander
4 bone-in pork rib chops (1 inch thick; about 2½ pounds total)

▶ Set the racks in the upper and lower thirds of oven. Heat oven to 400° F. On a rimmed baking sheet, toss the carrots and onion with 2 tablespoons of the oil and ¼ teaspoon each salt and pepper. Roast on the lower rack, tossing once, until tender, 25 to 28 minutes.

▶ Meanwhile, in a small bowl, combine the cranberries, preserves, and coriander. Using a paring knife, cut a 3-inch-deep pocket in the side of each chop and stuff with the mixture.

▶ Heat the remaining tablespoon of oil in a large ovenproof skillet over medium-high heat. Season the pork with ½ teaspoon each salt and pepper and cook until browned, 2 to 3 minutes per side. Transfer the skillet to oven (on the upper rack) and roast the pork until cooked through, 6 to 8 minutes. Serve with the carrots.

TIP
Try this recipe with boneless, skinless chicken breasts. The cooking time and temperature will be the same.

sausages with smashed potatoes and cornichons

hands-on time: 25 minutes / total time: 25 minutes / serves 4

1½ pounds red new potatoes
    (about 18), halved
    Kosher salt and black pepper
3 tablespoons olive oil
8 Italian sausage links (about
   1½ pounds total)
½ cup cornichons, chopped,
   plus 3 tablespoons of
   the brine
2 teaspoons Dijon mustard
½ small sweet onion (such
   as Vidalia or Walla Walla),
   chopped
¼ cup chopped fresh flat-leaf
   parsley

▶ Place the potatoes in a large pot and add enough cold water to cover. Bring to a boil and add 2 teaspoons salt. Reduce heat and simmer until tender, 15 to 18 minutes; drain.

▶ Meanwhile, heat 1 tablespoon of the oil in a large skillet over medium-high heat. Add the sausages and cook, turning occasionally, until browned and cooked through, 10 to 12 minutes.

▶ In a large bowl, whisk together the cornichon brine, mustard, the remaining 2 tablespoons of oil, and ¼ teaspoon each salt and pepper. Add the potatoes, cornichons, onion, and parsley and mix, mashing gently. Cut the sausages into large pieces and serve with the potatoes.

TIP
Cornichons are tiny, tart French-style pickles. Try them chopped in egg salad, sliced on a ham sandwich, or whole as an accompaniment to pâté, dried sausage, or smoked fish.

fennel-crusted pork with roasted root vegetables

hands-on time: 25 minutes / total time: 1 hour / serves 4

¾ pound carrots, peeled and cut into 3-inch sticks

¾ pound parsnips, peeled and cut into 3-inch sticks

1 medium red onion, cut into ½-inch wedges

2 tablespoons plus 2 teaspoons olive oil

Kosher salt and black pepper

1 pork tenderloin (about 1¼ pounds)

2 tablespoons fennel seeds, crushed

¾ cup apple cider

2 teaspoons honey

▶ Heat oven to 400° F. On a large rimmed baking sheet, toss the carrots, parsnips, and onion with 2 tablespoons of the oil, ½ teaspoon salt, and ¼ teaspoon pepper. Roast for 20 minutes.

▶ Meanwhile, season the pork with ½ teaspoon salt and ¼ teaspoon pepper and coat with the fennel seeds. Heat the remaining 2 teaspoons of oil in a large skillet over medium-high heat. Cook the pork, turning occasionally, until browned, 6 to 8 minutes.

▶ Transfer the pork to the baking sheet with the vegetables and roast until the internal temperature of the pork registers 145° F and the vegetables are tender, 16 to 20 minutes. Let the pork rest for at least 5 minutes before slicing.

▶ Meanwhile, wipe out the skillet, add the cider and honey, and whisk to combine. Boil until reduced by half, 4 to 6 minutes. Serve with the pork and vegetables.

TIP
To crush the fennel seeds, place them in a resealable plastic freezer bag and lightly pound them with a rolling pin, a meat mallet, or the bottom of a heavy skillet.

slow-cooker sweet and spicy Asian pork shoulder

hands-on time: 15 minutes / total time: 4½ to 8½ hours / serves 4

½ cup low-sodium soy sauce
½ cup brown sugar
1 to 2 tablespoons Asian chili-garlic sauce
1 tablespoon grated fresh ginger
1 teaspoon Chinese five-spice powder (optional)
 Kosher salt and black pepper
2½ pounds boneless pork shoulder, trimmed and cut into 2-inch pieces
1 cup long-grain white rice
1 medium head bok choy, thinly sliced (about 8 cups)
2 scallions, sliced

▶ In a 4- to 6-quart slow cooker, combine the soy sauce, brown sugar, chili-garlic sauce, ginger, five-spice powder (if using), ½ teaspoon salt, and ¼ teaspoon pepper. Add the pork and toss to coat. Cook, covered, until the pork is tender, on high for 4 to 5 hours or on low for 7 to 8 hours.

▶ Twenty-five minutes before serving, cook the rice according to the package directions.

▶ Once the pork is tender, skim off and discard any fat. If the slow cooker is on the low setting, turn it to high. Gently fold in the bok choy and cook, covered, until heated through, 2 to 4 minutes more. Serve with the rice and sprinkle with the scallions.

TIP
Sold in the spice aisle of many supermarkets, Chinese five-spice powder is typically made from a combination of cinnamon, cloves, fennel seed, star anise, and Szechuan peppercorns. Delicious in braised dishes, it also wakes up stir-fries and grilled meats.

dinner tonight:
seafood

salmon with brown butter, almonds, and green beans

hands-on time: 20 minutes / total time: 20 minutes / serves 4

4 tablespoons unsalted butter
1¼ pounds skinless salmon
   fillet, cut into 4 pieces
   Kosher salt and black pepper
1 pound green beans, trimmed
   and halved crosswise
¼ cup sliced almonds
2 tablespoons capers

▸ Heat 1 tablespoon of the butter in a large nonstick skillet over medium heat. Season the salmon with ½ teaspoon salt and ¼ teaspoon pepper. Cook until opaque throughout, 3 to 5 minutes per side; transfer to plates.

▸ Meanwhile, fill a second large skillet with ½ inch of water, bring to a boil, and add ¼ teaspoon salt. Add the green beans, cover, and cook until just tender, 4 to 5 minutes; drain and transfer to plates.

▸ Wipe out the second skillet and heat the remaining 3 tablespoons of butter over medium heat. Add the almonds and cook, stirring frequently, until both the almonds and the butter are golden brown (but not burned), 2 to 3 minutes. Stir in the capers. Spoon over the salmon and green beans.

TIP
The green beans with brown butter and almonds make an easy, impressive side dish for almost anything. Try them with roasted chicken or grilled steak.

creamy rice with roasted shrimp and tomatoes

hands-on time: 15 minutes / total time: 35 minutes / serves 4

2 tablespoons olive oil
1 onion, finely chopped
1 cup Arborio rice
1 cup dry white wine
   Kosher salt and black pepper
1 pound peeled and deveined
   medium shrimp
2 pints grape tomatoes
8 sprigs fresh thyme
2 cloves garlic, sliced

▶ Heat oven to 400° F. Heat 1 tablespoon of the oil in a large saucepan over medium heat. Add the onion and cook until soft, 5 to 7 minutes. Add the rice and wine and cook, stirring, until the wine is absorbed, 1 to 2 minutes.

▶ Add 2 cups water and ¼ teaspoon each salt and pepper to the saucepan. Simmer, covered, until the water is absorbed and the rice is tender, 18 to 20 minutes.

▶ Meanwhile, on a rimmed baking sheet, toss the shrimp, tomatoes, thyme, and garlic with the remaining tablespoon of oil and ½ teaspoon each salt and pepper. Roast until the shrimp are opaque throughout, 15 to 20 minutes. Serve over the rice.

TIP
Don't have Arborio rice? Serve the shrimp and tomatoes over long-grain white rice (cooked according to the package directions).

ginger-glazed cod with sautéed summer squash
hands-on time: 10 minutes / total time: 20 minutes / serves 4

2 tablespoons brown sugar

1 tablespoon low-sodium soy sauce

2 teaspoons grated fresh ginger

4 6-ounce pieces skinless cod, halibut, or striped bass fillet

2 tablespoons plus 1 teaspoon canola oil

Kosher salt and black pepper

1½ pounds small zucchini and summer squash (about 4 total), thinly sliced

¼ teaspoon crushed red pepper

¼ cup torn fresh mint leaves

▶ Heat broiler. In a small bowl, combine the brown sugar, soy sauce, and ginger; set aside.

▶ Place the cod on a foil-lined broilerproof rimmed baking sheet. Drizzle with 1 teaspoon of the oil and season with ¼ teaspoon each salt and black pepper. Broil until the cod is opaque throughout, 5 to 7 minutes, basting with the soy mixture twice during the last 2 minutes of cooking.

▶ Meanwhile, heat the remaining 2 tablespoons of oil in a large skillet over medium-high heat. Add the zucchini, squash, red pepper, and ½ teaspoon salt and cook, tossing frequently, until just tender, 5 to 7 minutes. Fold in the mint. Serve with the cod.

TIP
Have leftover ginger you won't be using soon? Peel it and pop it in the freezer. The next time you need it, just grate the frozen root. (A rasp grater works best.)

salmon kebabs with cilantro sauce

hands-on time: 15 minutes / total time: 25 minutes / serves 4

2   tablespoons pine nuts
1¼ pounds skinless salmon
     fillet, cut into 1½-inch pieces
     Kosher salt and black pepper
¼   cup olive oil
¼   cup chopped fresh cilantro
2   teaspoons grated lemon zest
4   pieces lavash bread

▶ Soak 16 wooden skewers in water for 10 minutes. Heat grill to medium-high. Heat oven to 350° F.

▶ Spread the pine nuts on a rimmed baking sheet and toast, tossing occasionally, until golden brown, 4 to 6 minutes. Let cool, then chop.

▶ Meanwhile, thread the salmon onto pairs of skewers and season with ½ teaspoon salt and ¼ teaspoon pepper. Grill, turning occasionally, until opaque throughout, 4 to 6 minutes.

▶ In a small bowl, combine the oil, cilantro, lemon zest, and pine nuts. Serve the salmon with the sauce and lavash.

TIP
Using 2 skewers instead of one prevents the salmon from turning and sliding during grilling. Try this with all types of kebabs.

creamy shrimp with corn and poblanos

hands-on time: 20 minutes / total time: 20 minutes / serves 4

1 cup long-grain white rice
1 tablespoon olive oil
2 poblano peppers, seeded
  and cut into $1/2$-inch pieces
$1\frac{1}{2}$ pounds peeled and deveined
  large shrimp
1 cup frozen corn
$3/4$ cup heavy cream
  Kosher salt and black pepper

▶ Cook the rice according to the package directions.

▶ Meanwhile, heat the oil in a large skillet over medium heat. Add the poblanos and cook, stirring occasionally, until tender, 5 to 6 minutes.

▶ Add the shrimp, corn, cream, $1/2$ teaspoon salt, and $1/4$ teaspoon black pepper to the skillet. Simmer until the shrimp are opaque throughout, 3 to 5 minutes. Serve over the rice.

TIP
Long, narrow poblanos have a slow, subtle heat. In a pinch, use a combination of 1 green bell pepper and 1 jalapeño pepper instead of the poblanos in this recipe.

tilapia with watercress and mango salad

hands-on time: 20 minutes / total time: 20 minutes / serves 4

¼ cup plus 2 teaspoons olive oil
4 tilapia fillets (about
   1¼ pounds total), halved
   lengthwise
   Kosher salt and black pepper
2 tablespoons fresh lime juice
2 teaspoons honey
2 teaspoons grated fresh ginger
¼ teaspoon crushed red pepper
6 cups watercress (from
   1 to 2 bunches), thick stems
   removed
1 mango, cut into small pieces
½ medium red onion, thinly
   sliced

▶ Heat 1 teaspoon of the oil in a large nonstick skillet over medium-high heat. Season the tilapia with ½ teaspoon salt and ¼ teaspoon black pepper. Add half the tilapia and cook until opaque throughout, 1 to 2 minutes per side. Transfer to a plate and repeat with 1 teaspoon of the remaining oil and the remaining tilapia.

▶ In a small bowl, whisk together the lime juice, honey, ginger, red pepper, the remaining ¼ cup of oil, and ¼ teaspoon each salt and black pepper.

▶ Divide the watercress, mango, onion, and tilapia among plates and drizzle with the dressing.

TIP
If you can't find a ripe mango in the produce aisle of your supermarket, try the fruit section of the salad bar.

Dijon salmon cakes with couscous

hands-on time: 15 minutes / total time: 15 minutes / serves 4

1 10-ounce package couscous
   (1½ cups)
½ cup kalamata olives, halved
¼ cup torn fresh mint leaves
2 tablespoons olive oil
   Kosher salt and black pepper
1 pound skinless salmon fillet
2 scallions, chopped
¼ cup panko bread crumbs
2 tablespoons Dijon mustard

▶ Cook the couscous according to the package directions. Fold in the olives, mint, 1 tablespoon of the oil, and ¼ teaspoon each salt and pepper.

▶ Meanwhile, in a food processor, combine the salmon, scallions, ½ teaspoon salt, and ¼ teaspoon pepper; pulse until coarsely chopped. Transfer to a medium bowl, mix in the bread crumbs and mustard, and form into 8 patties.

▶ Heat the remaining tablespoon of oil in a large nonstick skillet over medium heat. Cook the patties until opaque throughout, 2 to 3 minutes per side. Serve with the couscous.

TIP
The patties can be shaped up to 1 day in advance. Refrigerate them (uncooked), covered.

halibut with tomatoes and capers

hands-on time: 10 minutes / total time: 25 minutes / serves 4

1 tablespoon plus 1 teaspoon
  olive oil
2 cloves garlic, sliced
1 pint grape tomatoes, halved
½ cup fresh orange juice
2 tablespoons capers
  Kosher salt and black pepper
½ cup fresh flat-leaf parsley
  leaves
4 6-ounce pieces skinless
  halibut, cod, or striped
  bass fillet

▶ Heat 1 tablespoon of the oil in a large skillet over medium-high heat. Add the garlic and cook, stirring, until fragrant, about 30 seconds. Add the tomatoes, orange juice, capers, ½ teaspoon salt, and ¼ teaspoon pepper and simmer until some of the tomatoes begin to break down, 4 to 5 minutes. Stir in the parsley.

▶ Meanwhile, heat the remaining teaspoon of oil in a large nonstick skillet over medium-high heat. Season the halibut with ¼ teaspoon each salt and pepper. Cook until opaque throughout, 3 to 5 minutes per side. Serve with the tomato mixture.

TIP
Not a fan of capers? Use chopped kalamata olives instead.

shrimp potpie with fennel

hands-on time: 20 minutes / total time: 45 minutes / serves 4

3 tablespoons olive oil

2 leeks (white and light green parts), halved lengthwise and thinly sliced crosswise

1 fennel bulb, cut into ½-inch pieces

3 tablespoons all-purpose flour

½ cup dry white wine

1 cup whole milk
Kosher salt and black pepper

1 pound peeled and deveined medium shrimp

¼ cup chopped fresh flat-leaf parsley

1 sheet frozen puff pastry (half a 17.3-ounce package), thawed

▶ Heat oven to 400° F. Heat the oil in a large saucepan over medium-high heat. Cook the leeks and fennel, stirring occasionally, until soft, 5 to 6 minutes.

▶ Add the flour and cook for 1 minute, stirring (do not let it darken). Add the wine, milk, 1¼ teaspoons salt, and ¼ teaspoon pepper and simmer until thickened, 2 to 3 minutes. Stir in the shrimp and parsley.

▶ Transfer the mixture to a shallow 2-quart baking dish. Lay the pastry on top, trimming to fit, and cut vents in it. Bake until the shrimp mixture is bubbling and the pastry is golden brown, 25 to 30 minutes.

TIP
This is an excellent make-ahead dish for entertaining. The sauce can be prepared up to 8 hours in advance. Let it cool, then mix in the shrimp and parsley. Transfer the mixture to the baking dish, top with the pastry, and refrigerate, covered, until ready to bake.

curry-roasted salmon with tomatoes

hands-on time: 20 minutes / total time: 20 minutes / serves 4

1 cup long-grain white rice
1 pint grape tomatoes
1 tablespoon olive oil
  Kosher salt and black pepper
1¼ pounds skinless salmon fillet
2 teaspoons curry powder
¼ cup torn fresh basil leaves

▶ Heat oven to 400° F. Cook the rice according to the package directions.

▶ Meanwhile, on a rimmed baking sheet, toss the tomatoes with the oil and ¼ teaspoon each salt and pepper.

▶ Nestle the salmon in the tomatoes. Season with the curry powder, ½ teaspoon salt, and ¼ teaspoon pepper. Roast until the salmon is opaque throughout, 15 to 18 minutes.

▶ Serve the salmon and tomatoes over the rice and sprinkle with the basil.

TIP

For an easy next-day lunch, flake any leftover salmon and fold it into the rice. Serve it at room temperature with a dollop of yogurt and a squeeze of lime.

parchment-baked halibut with spinach and basil

hands-on time: 15 minutes / total time: 25 minutes / serves 4

4 6-ounce pieces skinless
   halibut, cod, or
   striped bass fillet
   Kosher salt and black pepper
12 sprigs fresh thyme
1 small orange, thinly sliced
2 tablespoons olive oil
1 10-ounce package spinach,
   thick stems removed
   (about 16 cups)
2 cups fresh basil leaves

▶ Heat oven to 400° F. Place the halibut on one side of each of four 12- to 15-inch lengths of parchment. Season with ½ teaspoon salt and ¼ teaspoon pepper. Top with the thyme and orange slices.

▶ Fold the parchment over the halibut and make small overlapping folds along the edges to seal, forming 4 packets. Transfer the packets to 2 baking sheets and bake for 12 minutes.

▶ Meanwhile, heat the oil in a large skillet over medium-high heat. Add the spinach, basil, and ¼ teaspoon each salt and pepper. Cook, tossing frequently, until just wilted, 2 to 3 minutes.

▶ Carefully cut open the packets and serve with the spinach.

TIP
Cooking food in parchment is a great way to cut down on fat. Try this recipe with different combinations of citrus and herbs.

seared scallops with snow peas and orange

hands-on time: 25 minutes / total time: 25 minutes / serves 4

1 cup couscous

1 tablespoon plus 2 teaspoons olive oil

16 sea scallops (about 1½ pounds)
   Kosher salt and black pepper

4 strips orange zest (removed with a vegetable peeler), thinly sliced

¾ pound snow peas, trimmed and halved lengthwise

▶ Cook the couscous according to the package directions.

▶ Meanwhile, heat 2 teaspoons of the oil in a large nonstick skillet over medium-high heat. Pat the scallops dry, season with ¼ teaspoon each salt and pepper, and cook until opaque throughout, 2 to 3 minutes per side. Transfer to a plate and cover to keep warm. Wipe out the skillet.

▶ Heat the remaining tablespoon of oil in the skillet over medium-high heat. Add the orange zest, snow peas, and ¼ teaspoon each salt and pepper and cook, tossing frequently, until the snow peas are just tender, about 2 minutes. Serve with the scallops and couscous.

TIP
Some scallops arrive in the store with the muscle still attached. A quick tug with your fingers removes it easily.

239

roasted salmon and peppers with caper vinaigrette

hands-on time: 10 minutes / total time: 25 minutes / serves 4

1 cup long-grain white rice
2 small red bell peppers,
   quartered
1 fennel bulb, thinly sliced
2 tablespoons olive oil
   Kosher salt and black pepper
1¼ pounds skinless salmon fillet
2 tablespoons chopped fresh
   flat-leaf parsley
1 tablespoon capers
1 tablespoon red wine vinegar

▶ Heat oven to 400° F. Cook the rice according to the package directions.

▶ Meanwhile, in a large roasting pan, toss the bell peppers and fennel with 1 tablespoon of the oil, ½ teaspoon salt, and ¼ teaspoon black pepper. Roast for 5 minutes.

▶ Season the salmon with ¼ teaspoon salt and ⅛ teaspoon black pepper and nestle it in the vegetables. Roast until the salmon is opaque throughout and the vegetables are just tender, 14 to 16 minutes more.

▶ In a small bowl, combine the parsley, capers, vinegar, and the remaining tablespoon of oil. Serve the salmon and vegetables with the rice and drizzle with the vinaigrette.

TIP
This is a great dish to serve at room temperature on a buffet. (Omit the rice.) The salmon, vegetables, and dressing can be prepared up to 1 day in advance; refrigerate separately, covered. Bring to room temperature and drizzle the fish with the dressing just before serving.

241

mussels with pesto and garlic oven fries

hands-on time: 15 minutes / total time: 40 minutes / serves 4

2 pounds russet potatoes (about 4 medium), cut into ¼-inch-thick sticks

4 garlic cloves, smashed

2 tablespoons olive oil
   Kosher salt and black pepper

1 cup dry white wine

2 pounds mussels, scrubbed

½ cup pesto

▶ Heat oven to 425° F. On a rimmed baking sheet, toss the potatoes and garlic with the oil, ¾ teaspoon salt, and ¼ teaspoon pepper.

▶ Roast the potatoes, turning once, until golden brown and crisp, 30 to 35 minutes.

▶ When the potatoes have 5 minutes left to cook, in a large pot bring the wine to a boil. Add the mussels and simmer, covered, until they open, 3 to 4 minutes. (Discard any that remain closed.) Transfer the mussels to bowls. Mix the pesto into the cooking liquid and spoon over the mussels. Serve with the oven fries.

TIP
Dry vermouth is a tasty substitute for white wine in this and other recipes. Try it the next time you want to avoid opening a bottle of white wine for cooking. (An opened bottle of vermouth will last for months in the refrigerator.)

shrimp and bacon with Cheddar grits

hands-on time: 20 minutes / total time: 20 minutes / serves 4

1 cup grits
4 ounces Cheddar, grated
   (1 cup)
4 slices bacon, cut into
   ½-inch pieces
1 pound peeled and deveined
   medium shrimp
2 plum tomatoes, chopped
2 scallions, sliced

▶ Cook the grits according to the package directions. Stir in the Cheddar.

▶ Meanwhile, cook the bacon in a large skillet over medium heat until crisp, 6 to 8 minutes. With a slotted spoon, transfer to a paper towel–lined plate.

▶ Add the shrimp and tomatoes to the bacon drippings in the skillet and cook, tossing occasionally, until the shrimp are opaque throughout, 3 to 5 minutes. Fold in the scallions and bacon and serve over the grits.

TIP
For a spicy New Orleans accent, try sliced andouille sausage in place of the bacon.

honey-soy glazed salmon with spinach and peppers

hands-on time: 20 minutes / total time: 20 minutes / serves 4

1 tablespoon honey
3 teaspoons low-sodium soy sauce
1¼ pounds skinless salmon fillet, cut into 4 pieces
Kosher salt and black pepper
1 tablespoon canola oil
1 red bell pepper, thinly sliced
1 tablespoon chopped fresh ginger
3 bunches flat-leaf spinach, thick stems removed (about 12 cups)
1 tablespoon toasted sesame seeds

▶ Heat broiler. In a small bowl, combine the honey and 1 teaspoon of the soy sauce.

▶ Place the salmon on a foil-lined broilerproof rimmed baking sheet and season with ½ teaspoon salt and ¼ teaspoon black pepper. Broil for 5 minutes. Spoon the honey mixture over the salmon. Broil until the fish is opaque throughout, 2 to 5 minutes more.

▶ Meanwhile, heat the oil in a large skillet over medium-high heat. Add the bell pepper and cook, tossing occasionally, until just tender, 3 to 4 minutes. Stir in the ginger.

▶ Add the spinach and ½ teaspoon salt to the skillet and cook, tossing, until just wilted, 2 to 3 minutes. Add the remaining 2 teaspoons of soy sauce. Serve with the salmon and sprinkle with the sesame seeds.

TIP
Toasted sesame seeds are often available in the spice aisle. If you can't find them, make your own: Toast the seeds in a skillet over medium heat, tossing almost constantly, until just golden, 1 to 2 minutes. Watch them carefully, as they scorch easily.

curried shrimp rolls

hands-on time: 10 minutes / total time: 10 minutes / serves 4

¼ cup mayonnaise
 1 tablespoon fresh lemon juice
¾ teaspoon curry powder
   Kosher salt and black pepper
 1 pound cooked peeled and
   deveined large shrimp,
   coarsely chopped
 2 stalks celery, chopped
 1 cup chopped arugula
 4 hot dog buns, toasted

▶ In a medium bowl, whisk together the mayonnaise, lemon juice, curry powder, and ¼ teaspoon each salt and pepper.

▶ Add the shrimp, celery, and arugula to the bowl and toss to combine. Serve in the buns.

TIP
If you're feeling indulgent, butter the buns inside and out and cook in a skillet, pressing occasionally, until golden brown.

ancho-rubbed salmon with summer squash

hands-on time: 20 minutes / total time: 20 minutes / serves 4

1 tablespoon brown sugar

1½ teaspoons ground ancho chili pepper
Kosher salt and black pepper

1¼ pounds skinless salmon fillet, cut into 4 pieces

2 tablespoons olive oil

1½ pounds small summer squash (about 4), thinly sliced

2 scallions, sliced

▶ Heat oven to 400° F. In a small bowl, combine the brown sugar, ancho chili, and ½ teaspoon salt.

▶ Place the salmon on a foil-lined rimmed baking sheet and drizzle with 1 tablespoon of the oil. Rub with the sugar mixture and roast until opaque throughout, 12 to 15 minutes.

▶ Meanwhile, heat the remaining tablespoon of oil in a large skillet over medium-high heat. Add the squash, ½ teaspoon salt, and ¼ teaspoon black pepper and cook, tossing occasionally, until just tender and beginning to brown, 5 to 7 minutes. Fold in the scallions. Serve with the salmon.

TIP
Take this recipe outside in summer. Grill the squash (halved lengthwise) and the salmon over medium-high heat until the squash is tender and the salmon is opaque throughout, 3 to 5 minutes per side. Slice the squash and toss with the scallions, oil, salt, and pepper.

tilapia with peppers and olives

hands-on time: 20 minutes / total time: 20 minutes / serves 4

2 tablespoons olive oil
4 6-ounce tilapia fillets
  Kosher salt and black pepper
2 red bell peppers, thinly sliced
1 onion, thinly sliced
½ cup pitted green olives
¼ cup chopped fresh flat-leaf
  parsley
2 tablespoons fresh lime juice

▶ Heat 1 tablespoon of the oil in a large nonstick skillet over medium-high heat. Season the tilapia with ¼ teaspoon each salt and black pepper and cook until opaque throughout, 4 to 5 minutes per side.

▶ Meanwhile, heat the remaining tablespoon of oil in a second large skillet over medium-high heat. Cook the bell peppers and onion, stirring often, until tender, 8 to 10 minutes. Stir in the olives, parsley, lime juice, and ¼ teaspoon each salt and black pepper. Serve with the tilapia.

TIP
Turn this dish into family-friendly fish tacos: Cut the tilapia into bite-size pieces before cooking (reduce the cooking time accordingly) and serve in warm corn tortillas with the vegetables.

grilled shrimp with lemony potato salad

hands-on time: 15 minutes / total time: 25 minutes / serves 4

1 pound red new potatoes
  (about 12)
  Kosher salt and black pepper
¼ cup sour cream
2 tablespoons fresh lemon
  juice
4 stalks celery, thinly sliced
2 tablespoons chopped fresh
  chives
½ pound asparagus, trimmed
2 tablespoons olive oil
1½ pounds medium shell-on
  shrimp
1 tablespoon seafood
  seasoning (such as Old Bay)

▶ Place the potatoes in a medium saucepan and add enough cold water to cover. Bring to a boil and add 2 teaspoons salt. Reduce heat and simmer until tender, 12 to 15 minutes. Drain, run under cold water to cool, and cut into quarters.

▶ In a large bowl, whisk together the sour cream, lemon juice, ¾ teaspoon salt, and ¼ teaspoon pepper. Add the potatoes, celery, and chives and toss to combine.

▶ Meanwhile, heat grill to medium-high. In a medium bowl, toss the asparagus with 1 tablespoon of the oil and ¼ teaspoon each salt and pepper. In a second medium bowl, toss the shrimp with the seafood seasoning and the remaining tablespoon of oil.

▶ Grill the asparagus, turning occasionally, until tender, 6 to 8 minutes. Grill the shrimp, turning, until opaque throughout, 2 to 4 minutes. Serve the shrimp and asparagus with the potato salad.

TIP
Grilling shrimp with the shells on keeps them moist and adds flavor. Many markets carry "easy peel" shrimp. Sliced along the back and deveined, they are a cinch to shell at the table.

salmon, black bean, and corn tostadas

hands-on time: 20 minutes / total time: 20 minutes / serves 4

1	tablespoon olive oil
1¼	pounds skinless salmon fillet, cut into 4 pieces
	Kosher salt and black pepper
4	tostada shells
1	cup black beans, rinsed
1	cup frozen corn kernels, thawed
1½	cups shredded romaine lettuce
½	cup jarred salsa verde (tomatillo salsa)
1	lime, cut into wedges

▶ Heat the oil in a large skillet over medium heat. Season the salmon with ½ teaspoon salt and ¼ teaspoon pepper and cook until opaque throughout, 5 to 6 minutes per side. Using a fork, flake the salmon.

▶ Dividing evenly, top the tostada shells with the salmon, beans, corn, lettuce, and salsa verde. Serve with the lime wedges.

TIP
Experiment with the toppings for this dish. Try avocado, radishes, and chopped red onion in addition to (or instead of) the toppings specified in the recipe.

257

hoisin-glazed shrimp skewers with cucumber salad

hands-on time: 15 minutes / total time: 15 minutes / serves 4

1 English cucumber, thinly
  sliced
2 scallions, sliced
2 tablespoons rice vinegar
2 tablespoons canola oil
  Kosher salt and black pepper
1 pound peeled and deveined
  medium shrimp
¼ cup hoisin sauce
2 teaspoons toasted sesame
  seeds

▶ Heat broiler. In a medium bowl, combine the cucumber, scallions, vinegar, oil, and ¼ teaspoon each salt and pepper and toss to combine.

▶ Thread the shrimp onto skewers, wrap the skewer ends with foil, and place on a foil-lined broilerproof rimmed baking sheet. Broil, basting often with the hoisin sauce, until opaque throughout, 2 to 3 minutes per side.

▶ Sprinkle the shrimp with the sesame seeds and serve with the cucumber salad.

TIP
Since shrimp are almost always shipped frozen, then defrosted before they hit the seafood case, you can save money and be better assured of freshness by buying bagged frozen shrimp.

salmon with warm lentil salad

hands-on time: 30 minutes / total time: 30 minutes / serves 4

1 cup green lentils, rinsed
  Kosher salt and black pepper
2 tablespoons plus 1 teaspoon
  olive oil
1¼ pounds skinless salmon
  fillet, cut into 4 pieces
2 tablespoons red wine vinegar
2 teaspoons Dijon mustard
¼ red onion, chopped
½ cup chopped fresh flat-leaf
  parsley
1 bunch arugula, thick stems
  removed and leaves torn
  (about 4 cups)
1 lemon, cut into wedges

▶ Bring 4 cups water to a boil. Add the lentils and 1 teaspoon salt and simmer, stirring occasionally, until tender, 20 to 25 minutes; drain.

▶ Meanwhile, heat 1 teaspoon of the oil in a large nonstick skillet over medium-high heat. Season the salmon with ¼ teaspoon each salt and pepper and cook until opaque throughout, 4 to 5 minutes per side.

▶ In a large bowl, combine the vinegar, mustard, onion, parsley, the remaining 2 tablespoons of oil, and ¼ teaspoon each salt and pepper.

▶ Add the lentils and arugula to the vinaigrette and toss to combine. Serve with the salmon and lemon.

TIP
Quick cooking and tasty, lentils are low in fat and rich in protein, fiber, iron, and folate. Leftovers make an excellent next-day lunch.

dinner tonight:
pasta

spaghetti with zucchini, walnuts, and raisins

hands-on time: 15 minutes / total time: 20 minutes / serves 4

12 ounces spaghetti (³⁄₄ box)
 3 tablespoons olive oil
 ¹⁄₂ cup walnut halves, roughly
    chopped
 4 cloves garlic, thinly sliced
1¹⁄₂ pounds small zucchini
    (4 to 5), halved lengthwise
    and sliced crosswise
 ³⁄₄ cup raisins
    Kosher salt and black pepper
 ¹⁄₄ cup grated Parmesan
    (1 ounce)

▶ Cook the pasta according to the package directions; drain and return it to the pot.

▶ Meanwhile, heat the oil in a large skillet over medium-high heat. Add the walnuts and cook, stirring frequently, until beginning to brown, 3 to 4 minutes. Add the garlic and cook, stirring, until beginning to brown, about 1 minute.

▶ Add the zucchini and raisins to the skillet, season with ¹⁄₂ teaspoon salt and ¹⁄₄ teaspoon pepper, and cook, tossing occasionally, until the zucchini is just tender, 4 to 5 minutes.

▶ Add the zucchini mixture to the pasta and toss to combine. Serve with the Parmesan.

TIP
Garlic can rapidly go from golden to scorched. Before placing it in the oil, have the zucchini sliced and ready to go. When the zucchini and raisins hit the pan, they will lower the temperature of the oil and keep the garlic from overcooking.

gnocchi with roasted cauliflower

hands-on time: 10 minutes / total time: 35 minutes / serves 4

1 small head cauliflower, cut
   into small florets
¼ cup fresh sage leaves
3 tablespoons olive oil
   Kosher salt and black pepper
1 pound gnocchi (fresh or
   frozen)
¼ cup grated Parmesan
   (1 ounce)

▶ Heat oven to 400° F. On a rimmed baking sheet, toss the cauliflower and sage with the oil, ½ teaspoon salt, and ¼ teaspoon pepper. Roast, tossing once, until the cauliflower is golden brown and tender, 25 to 30 minutes.

▶ Fifteen minutes before the cauliflower is finished, cook the gnocchi according to the package directions. Divide the gnocchi among bowls and top with the cauliflower and Parmesan.

TIP
Cauliflower florets are easier to separate if you remove the core first. Place the head stem-side up. Using a paring knife, cut around the core at an angle, creating a cone-shaped piece, then lift it out. (If the head is very large, halve it first through the core.)

pasta with chicken sausage and broccoli

hands-on time: 20 minutes / total time: 20 minutes / serves 4

12 ounces rigatoni ($^3/_4$ box)
1 tablespoon olive oil
1 onion, sliced
6 ounces fully cooked chicken
   sausage links, sliced
1 small bunch broccoli, cut into
   florets and stems sliced
$^1/_4$ cup grated Parmesan
   (1 ounce)

▶ Cook the pasta according to the package directions; drain and return it to the pot.

▶ Meanwhile, heat the oil in a large skillet over medium-high heat. Cook the onion, stirring frequently, until beginning to soften, 2 to 3 minutes. Add the sausage and cook, tossing, until browned, 2 to 3 minutes more.

▶ Add the broccoli and 1$^1/_4$ cups water to the skillet and simmer, covered, until the broccoli is tender, 5 to 6 minutes.

▶ Add the sausage mixture and Parmesan to the pasta and toss to combine.

TIP
Fully cooked chicken sausage links come in a number of tasty flavors. For this dish, try a roasted garlic or apple variety.

spinach and ricotta–stuffed shells

hands-on time: 20 minutes / total time: 45 minutes / serves 4

20 jumbo pasta shells (about
   half a 12-ounce box)
 1 24-ounce jar marinara sauce
 2 15-ounce containers ricotta
 2 cups baby spinach, chopped
½ cup grated Parmesan
   (2 ounces)
   Kosher salt and black pepper
 4 ounces mozzarella, grated
   (1 cup)
   Green salad (optional)

▶ Set an oven rack to the highest position and heat oven to 400° F. Cook the shells according to the package directions; drain and run under cold water to cool.

▶ Spread the marinara sauce in the bottom of a large broilerproof baking dish.

▶ In a bowl, combine the ricotta, spinach, Parmesan, ½ teaspoon salt, and ¼ teaspoon pepper. Spoon the mixture into the shells and place them on top of the sauce in the baking dish. Sprinkle with the mozzarella and bake until the shells are heated through, 10 to 12 minutes.

▶ Increase heat to broil. Broil the shells until the mozzarella begins to brown, 2 to 5 minutes. Serve with the salad, if desired.

TIP
Want to sneak an extra helping of green vegetables into this dish? Chop up cooked green beans, broccoli, or asparagus and fold it into the ricotta mixture along with the spinach.

spaghetti with shrimp, Feta, and dill

hands-on time: 25 minutes / total time: 25 minutes / serves 4

12 ounces spaghetti (³⁄₄ box)
¹⁄₄ cup plus 1 tablespoon
    olive oil
 1 pound peeled and deveined
    large shrimp
    Kosher salt and black pepper
 2 tablespoons fresh lemon juice
 1 teaspoon grated lemon zest
 3 ounces Feta, crumbled
    (³⁄₄ cup)
 2 tablespoons coarsely chopped
    fresh dill

▶ Cook the pasta according to the package directions; drain and return it to the pot.

▶ Meanwhile, heat 1 tablespoon of the oil in a large skillet over medium-high heat. Season the shrimp with ½ teaspoon salt and ¼ teaspoon pepper and cook, tossing occasionally, until opaque throughout, 3 to 4 minutes. Stir in the lemon juice and zest.

▶ Add the shrimp mixture to the pasta, along with the Feta, dill, the remaining ¼ cup of oil, and ¼ teaspoon each salt and pepper. Toss to combine.

TIP
Crumbled Feta sold in supermarkets can be dry, flavorless, and treated with additives that prevent caking. It's worth buying a block of cheese and crumbling it yourself.

ravioli with peas and crispy bacon

**hands-on time: 25 minutes / total time: 25 minutes
serves 4**

16 to 18 ounces cheese ravioli (fresh or frozen)
 6 slices bacon
 2 cloves garlic, sliced
 1 10-ounce package frozen peas
   Kosher salt and black pepper
 1 ounce ricotta salata, grated (¼ cup)

▶ Cook the pasta according to the package directions. Reserve ¼ cup of the cooking water and drain the pasta.

▶ Meanwhile, cook the bacon in a large skillet over medium heat until crisp, 6 to 8 minutes. Transfer to a paper towel–lined plate. Let cool, then break into pieces.

▶ Return the skillet to medium heat, add the garlic, and cook, stirring, until golden brown, 1 to 2 minutes. Add the peas and cook until heated through, 2 to 3 minutes.

▶ Add the pasta, the reserved cooking water, ½ teaspoon salt, and ¼ teaspoon pepper and toss. Sprinkle with the bacon and ricotta salata.

ravioli with brown butter and sage

**hands-on time: 10 minutes / total time: 25 minutes
serves 4**

16 to 18 ounces cheese ravioli (fresh or frozen)
 6 tablespoons unsalted butter (¾ stick)
¼ cup pine nuts
⅓ cup fresh sage leaves
   Kosher salt and black pepper

▶ Cook the pasta according to the package directions.

▶ Meanwhile, melt the butter in a large skillet over medium heat. Add the pine nuts and sage and cook, stirring occasionally, until the sage is crisp and the butter and pine nuts are browned (but not burned), 6 to 8 minutes.

▶ Add the pasta, ½ teaspoon salt, and ¼ teaspoon pepper to the skillet and toss to combine.

ravioli with grape tomatoes and wine

hands-on time: 25 minutes / total time: 25 minutes
serves 4

16 to 18 ounces cheese ravioli (fresh or frozen)
 2 tablespoons olive oil
 2 shallots, chopped
 1 pint grape tomatoes, halved
 1 cup dry white wine
    Kosher salt and black pepper
 2 tablespoons unsalted butter
¼ cup chopped fresh flat-leaf parsley

▶ Cook the pasta according to the package directions.

▶ Meanwhile, heat the oil in a large skillet over medium heat. Add the shallots and cook, stirring occasionally, until soft, 3 to 5 minutes. Add the tomatoes, wine, ½ teaspoon salt, and ¼ teaspoon pepper and simmer until the tomatoes begin to soften, 4 to 5 minutes.

▶ Add the pasta, butter, and parsley to the skillet and toss to combine.

creamy ravioli and pesto gratin

hands-on time: 10 minutes / total time: 40 minutes
serves 4

16 to 18 ounces cheese ravioli (fresh or frozen)
 1 cup heavy cream
¼ cup pesto
¼ cup grated Parmesan (1 ounce)

▶ Heat oven to 400° F. Cook the pasta according to the package directions.

▶ In a large bowl, whisk together the cream and pesto. Add the pasta and toss to combine.

▶ Transfer the mixture to a shallow 2-quart baking dish and sprinkle with the Parmesan. Bake until golden brown and bubbling, 20 to 25 minutes.

pasta with Brie, mushrooms, and arugula

hands-on time: 20 minutes / total time: 20 minutes / serves 4

12 ounces penne (³/₄ box)
1 tablespoon olive oil
1 pound button mushrooms, quartered
1 small red onion, sliced
½ cup dry white wine
   Kosher salt and black pepper
8 ounces Brie, cut into 1-inch pieces
4 cups baby arugula

▶ Cook the pasta according to the package directions. Reserve ½ cup of the cooking water; drain the pasta and return it to the pot.

▶ Meanwhile, heat the oil in a large skillet over medium-high heat. Add the mushrooms and onion and cook, tossing occasionally, until the mushrooms begin to release their juices, 2 to 3 minutes. Add the wine, ½ teaspoon salt, and ¼ teaspoon pepper and cook until the mushrooms begin to brown, 5 to 6 minutes more.

▶ Add the Brie and the reserved cooking water to the pasta and toss until coated. Fold in the mushroom mixture and arugula.

TIP
Mixing Brie with the pasta cooking water is a quick way to create a rich, creamy sauce. For best results, bring the Brie to room temperature before using.

spaghetti with sweet potatoes and ricotta

hands-on time: 25 minutes / total time: 25 minutes / serves 4

12 ounces spaghetti ($^3/_4$ box)
 2 tablespoons olive oil
 1 pound sweet potatoes
   (about 2), cut into $^1/_2$-inch
   pieces
   Kosher salt and black pepper
 2 shallots, sliced
 1 tablespoon chopped fresh
   rosemary
$^1/_4$ cup grated Parmesan
   (1 ounce)
$^1/_3$ cup ricotta

▸ Cook the pasta according to the package directions. Reserve ½ cup of the cooking water; drain the pasta and return it to the pot.

▸ Meanwhile, heat the oil in a large nonstick skillet over medium heat. Add the sweet potatoes, ¾ teaspoon salt, and ¼ teaspoon pepper and cook, covered, stirring occasionally, for 10 minutes.

▸ Add the shallots and rosemary to the skillet and cook, uncovered, stirring occasionally, until the potatoes are tender, 3 to 5 minutes more.

▸ Add the potato mixture, Parmesan, and the reserved cooking water to the pasta and toss to combine. Dollop with the ricotta before serving.

TIP
Butternut squash is a tasty alternative to the sweet potatoes in this creamy dish.

pappardelle with spicy meat sauce

hands-on time: 20 minutes / total time: 20 minutes / serves 4

12 ounces pappardelle
 1 tablespoon olive oil
 3/4 pound ground beef
 6 cloves garlic, chopped
 2 anchovy fillets
 1/4 teaspoon crushed red pepper
    Kosher salt and black pepper
 1 28-ounce can crushed
    tomatoes
 1/4 cup dry white wine
 1/2 cup grated Parmesan
    (2 ounces)

▶ Cook the pasta according to the package directions; drain and return it to the pot.

▶ Meanwhile, heat the oil in a large skillet over medium-high heat. Add the beef and cook, breaking it up with a spoon, until browned, 4 to 5 minutes. Stir in the garlic, anchovies, red pepper, 1/2 teaspoon salt, and 1/4 teaspoon black pepper.

▶ Add the tomatoes and wine to the skillet and simmer, stirring occasionally, until slightly thickened, 8 to 10 minutes.

▶ Add the sauce and 1/4 cup of the Parmesan to the pasta and toss to combine. Sprinkle with the remaining 1/4 cup of Parmesan before serving.

TIP
Pappardelle are flat, wide pasta noodles. If you can't find them, tagliatelle or fettuccine will also work in this recipe.

281

creamy pecorino pasta with radicchio salad

hands-on time: 25 minutes / total time: 25 minutes / serves 4

12 ounces spaghetti ($^3/_4$ box)
$^1/_2$ large head radicchio, sliced
   (about 2 cups)
$^3/_4$ cup pitted mixed olives
 3 tablespoons store-bought
   balsamic vinaigrette
   Kosher salt and black pepper
 1 cup heavy cream
$^1/_2$ cup grated pecorino
   (2 ounces), plus more for
   serving
$^1/_2$ teaspoon cracked black
   pepper, plus more for serving

▸ Cook the pasta according to the package directions; drain and return it to the pot.

▸ Meanwhile, in a large bowl, toss the radicchio and olives with the vinaigrette and ¼ teaspoon each salt and black pepper.

▸ Add the cream to the pasta and bring to a simmer. Add the pecorino, cracked black pepper, and ½ teaspoon salt and cook, tossing, until thickened and creamy, about 2 minutes.

▸ Top the pasta with additional pecorino and cracked black pepper and serve with the salad.

TIP
Radicchio has a peppery, slightly bitter taste. If you prefer to round out its flavor, add raisins or chopped fresh spinach to the salad.

rigatoni peperonata

hands-on time: 25 minutes / total time: 25 minutes / serves 4

¼ cup pine nuts

12 ounces rigatoni (¾ box)

¼ cup olive oil

3 bell peppers (preferably red and yellow), cut into ½-inch pieces

½ cup pitted kalamata olives, halved

¼ cup chopped fresh flat-leaf parsley

2 tablespoons chopped capers

2 tablespoons red wine vinegar

¼ teaspoon crushed red pepper
   Kosher salt and black pepper

▶ Heat oven to 400° F. Spread the pine nuts on a rimmed baking sheet and toast, tossing occasionally, until golden brown, 4 to 6 minutes. Cook the pasta according to the package directions.

▶ Meanwhile, heat the oil in a large skillet over medium-high heat. Add the bell peppers and cook, stirring occasionally, until tender, 5 to 6 minutes. Add the olives, parsley, capers, vinegar, crushed red pepper, and ¼ teaspoon each salt and black pepper and cook, stirring, until heated through, 1 to 2 minutes.

▶ Add the pasta and pine nuts to the skillet and cook, tossing, until heated through, 1 minute.

TIP
Peperonata, made with sautéed peppers and olive oil (and sometimes onions, garlic, and tomatoes), is a classic Mediterranean condiment. Cook a double batch and try it on crostini, layered in sandwiches, or as a topping for chicken, steak, or fish.

pasta with bacon and cauliflower

hands-on time: 30 minutes / total time: 30 minutes / serves 4

12 ounces spaghetti (³/₄ box)
6 slices bacon
¹/₃ cup fresh sage leaves
1 small head cauliflower
    (about 1¹/₂ pounds),
    cut into small florets
    Kosher salt and black pepper
³/₄ cup grated pecorino
    (3 ounces)

▶ Cook the pasta according to the package directions. Reserve ¾ cup of the cooking water; drain the pasta and return it to the pot.

▶ Meanwhile, cook the bacon in a large skillet over medium heat until crisp, 6 to 8 minutes; transfer to a paper towel–lined plate. Let cool, then break into pieces.

▶ Add the sage to the bacon drippings in the skillet and cook over medium heat, turning once, until crisp, 1 to 2 minutes; transfer to the paper towel–lined plate.

▶ Add the cauliflower, ¼ cup water, and ¼ teaspoon each salt and pepper to the skillet and cook, covered, for 2 minutes. Uncover and cook, tossing frequently, until golden and tender, 3 to 4 minutes more.

▶ Add the reserved cooking water and ½ cup of the pecorino to the pasta and toss until creamy. Add the cauliflower, sage, and bacon and toss to combine. Sprinkle with the remaining ¼ cup of pecorino before serving.

TIP
For maximum flavor, buy hard cheeses, like pecorino and Parmesan, in wedges and grate as needed. (They also last longer ungrated.)

lasagna with broccoli and three cheeses

hands-on time: 15 minutes / total time: 1 hour, 10 minutes / serves 4

1 15-ounce container ricotta

1 pound frozen broccoli florets—thawed, patted dry, and chopped

2¼ cups grated mozzarella (9 ounces)

½ cup grated Parmesan (2 ounces)

Kosher salt and black pepper

1 16-ounce jar marinara sauce

½ cup heavy cream

8 no-boil lasagna noodles

2 tablespoons olive oil, plus more for the foil

4 cups mixed greens

1 tablespoon fresh lemon juice

▶ Heat oven to 400° F. In a large bowl, combine the ricotta, broccoli, 2 cups of the mozzarella, ¼ cup of the Parmesan, ½ teaspoon salt, and ¼ teaspoon pepper. In a small bowl, combine the marinara sauce and cream.

▶ Spoon a thin layer of the sauce into the bottom of an 8-inch square baking dish. Top with 2 noodles, a quarter of the remaining sauce, and a third of the broccoli mixture; repeat twice. Top with the remaining 2 noodles and sauce. Sprinkle with the remaining ¼ cup of mozzarella and ¼ cup of Parmesan.

▶ Cover the lasagna tightly with an oiled piece of foil and bake until the noodles are tender, 35 to 40 minutes. Uncover and bake until golden brown, 10 to 15 minutes more.

▶ Toss the greens with the oil, lemon juice, and ¼ teaspoon each salt and pepper. Serve with the lasagna.

TIP
To help the lasagna hold together when it's cut, alternate the direction of the noodles in each layer.

289

fettuccine with lima beans, peas, and leeks

hands-on time: 25 minutes / total time: 25 minutes / serves 4

12 ounces fettuccine (³/₄ box)
 1 10-ounce package frozen
    lima beans (about 1¹/₂ cups)
 1 cup frozen peas
 2 tablespoons olive oil
 2 leeks (white and light green
    parts), halved lengthwise and
    sliced crosswise
    Kosher salt and black pepper
³/₄ cup heavy cream
 2 tablespoons chopped fresh
    tarragon
¹/₄ cup grated pecorino or
    Parmesan (1 ounce)

▶ Cook the pasta according to the package directions, adding the beans and peas during the last 2 minutes of cooking; drain.

▶ Meanwhile, heat the oil in a large skillet over medium heat. Add the leeks and season with ¹/₂ teaspoon salt and ¹/₄ teaspoon pepper. Cook, stirring occasionally, until tender (but not brown), 8 to 10 minutes. Add the cream and cook until slightly thickened, 3 to 4 minutes more.

▶ Add the pasta and tarragon to the skillet and toss to combine. Sprinkle with the pecorino before serving.

TIP
To clean leeks, fill a bowl with cold water, add the cut leeks, and swish them around a few times. With your hands loosely cupped, scoop up the leeks and place them on a plate. (The grit will be left behind in the bowl.) Discard the water and grit and repeat until the water remains clear.

dinner tonight:
vegetarian

eggplant lasagna with fresh basil

hands-on time: 20 minutes / total time: 50 minutes / serves 4

½ pound plum tomatoes, halved and seeded

1 clove garlic

4 tablespoons olive oil
Kosher salt and black pepper

2 eggplants (about 3 pounds), sliced lengthwise ¼ inch thick

1 cup ricotta

1 large egg

¼ cup chopped fresh basil

¼ cup grated Asiago or Parmesan (1 ounce)

4 cups mixed greens

▶ Heat broiler. In a food processor, puree the tomatoes and garlic with 1 tablespoon of the oil and ¼ teaspoon each salt and pepper.

▶ Arrange the eggplants on 2 broilerproof rimmed baking sheets, brush on both sides with 2 tablespoons of the remaining oil, and season with ½ teaspoon salt and ¼ teaspoon pepper. One sheet at a time, broil until charred and tender, 3 to 4 minutes per side.

▶ Meanwhile, in a small bowl, combine the ricotta, egg, basil, and ¼ teaspoon each salt and pepper.

▶ On the bottom of an 8-inch square baking dish, spread half the tomato sauce. Top with a third of the eggplant and half the ricotta mixture; repeat. Top with the remaining eggplant and tomato sauce and sprinkle with the Asiago.

▶ Reduce oven to 400° F. Bake the lasagna until bubbling, 15 to 20 minutes. Let rest for 10 minutes before serving.

▶ In a large bowl, toss the greens with the remaining tablespoon of oil and ¼ teaspoon each salt and pepper. Serve with the lasagna.

TIP
Eggplants are tastiest when less than 1½ pounds. And they should feel heavy for their size. Larger, older ones tend to be bitter.

tofu tacos with spinach, corn, and goat cheese

hands-on time: 20 minutes / total time: 20 minutes / serves 4

1 tablespoon olive oil
1 14-ounce package extra-firm tofu—drained, patted dry, and crumbled
1½ teaspoons chili powder
   Kosher salt and black pepper
1 10-ounce package frozen corn (2 cups)
6 cups baby spinach (about 5 ounces)
8 small flour tortillas, warmed
3 ounces fresh goat cheese, crumbled (¾ cup)
¾ cup store-bought fresh salsa

▶ Heat the oil in a large nonstick skillet over medium-high heat. Add the tofu, chili powder, ½ teaspoon salt, and ¼ teaspoon pepper and cook, tossing occasionally, until golden brown, 4 to 5 minutes.

▶ Add the corn to the skillet and cook, tossing, until heated through, 2 to 3 minutes. Add the spinach and ½ teaspoon each salt and pepper and toss until the spinach is wilted, 1 to 2 minutes.

▶ Fill the tortillas with the tofu mixture, goat cheese, and salsa.

TIP
To warm the tortillas, wrap a stack of them in foil and heat in a 350° F oven for 8 to 10 minutes.

poached eggs with mushrooms and tomatoes

hands-on time: 30 minutes / total time: 30 minutes / serves 4

2 teaspoons white vinegar
1 tablespoon plus 1 teaspoon olive oil
2 medium tomatoes, each sliced into 4 rounds
  Kosher salt and black pepper
1 pound assorted mushrooms, sliced
1 tablespoon fresh thyme leaves
8 large eggs
4 slices country bread, toasted
1 ounce Parmesan, shaved (¼ cup)
2 tablespoons chopped fresh chives

▶ Fill a large, deep skillet with 3 inches of water. Add the vinegar and bring to a bare simmer.

▶ Meanwhile, heat 1 teaspoon of the oil in a large nonstick skillet over medium-high heat. Season the tomatoes with ¼ teaspoon each salt and pepper and cook until just tender, 1 to 2 minutes per side; transfer to a plate.

▶ Add the remaining tablespoon of oil to the second skillet and heat over medium-high heat. Add the mushrooms, thyme, ½ teaspoon salt, and ¼ teaspoon pepper and cook, tossing occasionally, until the mushrooms are golden brown and tender, 6 to 7 minutes.

▶ Meanwhile, poach the eggs in 2 batches: One at a time, crack each egg into a small bowl and slide it gently into the water in the deep skillet. Cook 2 to 3 minutes for slightly runny yolks; remove with a slotted spoon.

▶ Top the bread with the tomatoes, mushrooms, eggs, and Parmesan. Season with ¼ teaspoon each salt and pepper and sprinkle with the chives.

TIP
The easiest way to create nice, thin shavings from a block of Parmesan is to use a vegetable peeler.

creamy barley with tomatoes and greens

hands-on time: 30 minutes / total time: 30 minutes / serves 4

2 tablespoons olive oil
1 large onion, finely chopped
  Kosher salt and black pepper
2 cups quick-cooking barley
1 28-ounce can diced
  tomatoes, drained
1 cup dry white wine
8 cups torn mustard green
  leaves (from 1 small bunch)
  or spinach
2 ounces Taleggio or Brie
  (rind removed), cut into
  small pieces
½ cup grated Parmesan
  (2 ounces)

▶ Heat the oil in a large saucepan over medium heat. Add the onion, ½ teaspoon salt, and ¼ teaspoon pepper and cook, stirring occasionally, until tender, 5 to 7 minutes.

▶ Add the barley, tomatoes, wine, and 2½ cups water to the saucepan and bring to a boil. Reduce heat and simmer, stirring occasionally, until the barley is tender, 12 to 15 minutes.

▶ Add the mustard greens, Taleggio, and ¼ cup of the Parmesan to the saucepan and cook, stirring occasionally, until the mustard greens are tender, 3 to 4 minutes more. Serve sprinkled with the remaining ¼ cup of Parmesan.

TIP
Quick-cooking barley can be used in most recipes that call for pearl barley. It tastes similar but cooks faster because it has been steamed.

pierogi with sautéed red cabbage

hands-on time: 20 minutes / total time: 20 minutes / serves 4

1 16-ounce box frozen
   potato-and-onion pierogi
1 tablespoon olive oil
1 onion, thinly sliced
½ small head red cabbage
   (about 1 pound), cored and
   thinly sliced
1 Granny Smith apple, cut
   into ½-inch pieces
2 tablespoons red wine vinegar
1 teaspoon caraway seeds
   Kosher salt and black pepper
2 tablespoons chopped fresh
   flat-leaf parsley
   Sour cream (optional)

▶ Cook the pierogi according to the package directions.

▶ Meanwhile, heat the oil in a medium skillet over medium heat. Add the onion and cook, stirring occasionally, until tender, 5 to 7 minutes.

▶ Add the cabbage, apple, vinegar, caraway seeds, ½ teaspoon salt, and ¼ teaspoon pepper to the skillet and cook, stirring, until the cabbage is slightly wilted but still crunchy, 4 to 5 minutes. Stir in the parsley. Serve with the pierogi and the sour cream, if desired.

TIP
Although pierogi (Eastern European dumplings) can be boiled, pan-frying them produces a crispy exterior that contrasts nicely with their creamy fillings.

spicy three-pepper pizza
**hands-on time: 10 minutes / total time: 40 minutes
serves 4**

- 1 pound pizza dough, thawed if frozen
  Cornmeal, for the pan
- ³/₄ cup marinara sauce
- 8 ounces Gruyère, grated (2 cups)
- 1 sliced red bell pepper
- 1 sliced poblano pepper
- 8 whole pepperoncini peppers
  Kosher salt and black pepper

▸ Heat oven to 425° F. Shape the dough into a large round and place on a cornmeal-dusted rimmed baking sheet.

▸ Top the dough with the marinara sauce, Gruyère, bell pepper, poblano pepper, and pepperoncini. Season with ⅛ teaspoon each salt and black pepper. Bake until golden brown, 25 to 30 minutes.

squash-Cheddar flat bread
**hands-on time: 15 minutes / total time: 45 minutes
serves 4**

- 1 pound pizza dough, thawed if frozen
  Cornmeal, for the pan
- 1 pound butternut squash—peeled, seeded, and sliced ¼ inch thick
- ½ red onion, thinly sliced
- ¼ cup pine nuts
- 1 tablespoon fresh thyme leaves
- 1 tablespoon olive oil
  Kosher salt and black pepper
- 6 ounces extra-sharp Cheddar, grated (1½ cups)

▸ Heat oven to 400° F. Shape the dough into a large oval and place on a cornmeal-dusted rimmed baking sheet.

▸ In a large bowl, toss the squash, onion, pine nuts, and thyme with the oil, ½ teaspoon salt, and ¼ teaspoon pepper. Scatter over the dough and sprinkle with the Cheddar. Bake until golden brown, 30 to 35 minutes.

tomato-olive pizza

hands-on time: 10 minutes / total time: 40 minutes
serves 4

1 pound pizza dough, thawed if frozen
  Cornmeal, for the pan
1 pound beefsteak tomatoes (about 2), thinly sliced
¼ cup pitted kalamata olives, halved
2 scallions, thinly sliced
2 tablespoons olive oil
  Black pepper

▶ Heat oven to 425° F. Shape the dough into
a large round and place on a cornmeal-dusted
rimmed baking sheet.

▶ Top the dough with the tomatoes, olives, and
scallions. Drizzle with the oil and season with
¼ teaspoon pepper. Bake until golden brown, 25
to 30 minutes.

potato-rosemary flat bread

hands-on time: 10 minutes / total time: 40 minutes
serves 4

1 pound pizza dough, thawed if frozen
  Cornmeal, for the pan
4 red new potatoes, thinly sliced
2 cloves garlic, thinly sliced
2 tablespoons fresh rosemary leaves
2 tablespoons olive oil
  Kosher salt and black pepper

▶ Heat oven to 425° F. Shape the dough into
a large oval and place on a cornmeal-dusted
rimmed baking sheet.

▶ In a large bowl, toss the potatoes, garlic, and
rosemary with the oil, ½ teaspoon salt, and
¼ teaspoon pepper. Scatter over the dough. Bake
until golden brown, 25 to 30 minutes.

stir-fried rice noodles with tofu and vegetables

hands-on time: 25 minutes / total time: 25 minutes / serves 4

1 8-ounce package rice noodles or 12 ounces linguine
¼ cup brown sugar
¼ cup low-sodium soy sauce
2 tablespoons fresh lime juice
1 14-ounce package firm tofu, sliced ½ inch thick
1 tablespoon canola oil
2 carrots, cut into thin strips
1 red bell pepper, thinly sliced
1 tablespoon grated fresh ginger
2 cups bean sprouts
4 scallions, thinly sliced
¼ cup roasted peanuts, roughly chopped
½ cup fresh cilantro sprigs

▶ Cook the noodles according to the package directions. Drain and return them to the pot.

▶ Meanwhile, in a small bowl, whisk together the sugar, soy sauce, and lime juice. Gently press the tofu slices between layers of paper towels to remove excess liquid, then cut into ½-inch pieces.

▶ Heat the oil in a large skillet over medium-high heat. Add the carrots, bell pepper, and ginger and cook, tossing frequently, for 2 minutes. Add the tofu and bean sprouts and cook, tossing occasionally, until the vegetables are slightly tender, 3 to 4 minutes more.

▶ Add half the soy sauce mixture to the noodles and cook over medium-high heat, tossing occasionally, until heated through, 1 to 2 minutes.

▶ Transfer the noodles to a platter. Top with the carrot mixture, scallions, peanuts, cilantro, and the remaining soy sauce mixture.

TIP
Cilantro sprigs can be used (or chopped) whole—there's no need to remove the sweet, tender stems.

quinoa with mushrooms, kale, and sweet potatoes

hands-on time: 15 minutes / total time: 30 minutes / serves 4

1 cup quinoa

2 tablespoons olive oil

1 pound small sweet potatoes
(about 2), peeled and cut
into ¾-inch pieces

10 ounces button mushrooms,
quartered

2 cloves garlic, thinly sliced

1 bunch kale, thick stems
removed and leaves torn
into 2-inch pieces

¾ cup dry white wine
Kosher salt and black pepper

¼ cup grated Parmesan
(1 ounce)

▶ Cook the quinoa according to the package directions.

▶ Meanwhile, heat the oil in a large pot over medium heat. Add the sweet potatoes and mushrooms and cook, tossing occasionally, until golden and beginning to soften, 5 to 6 minutes.

▶ Add the garlic and cook, stirring, for 1 minute. Add the kale, wine, ¾ teaspoon salt, and ¼ teaspoon pepper. Cook, tossing often, until the vegetables are tender, 10 to 12 minutes more. Serve over the quinoa and sprinkle with the Parmesan.

TIP
Quinoa is a quick-cooking whole grain that's slightly nutty tasting and packed with protein. It's stocked near the rice in many supermarkets. If you can't find it, barley and bulgur are tasty substitutes in this recipe.

skillet-poached huevos rancheros

hands-on time: 15 minutes / total time: 15 minutes / serves 4

1 16-ounce jar salsa (2 cups)
1 15.5-ounce can black beans, rinsed
4 large eggs
  Kosher salt and black pepper
2 scallions, sliced
¼ cup chopped fresh cilantro
4 small flour tortillas, warmed
½ cup sour cream

▶ In a large skillet, combine the salsa and beans and bring to a simmer.

▶ Make 4 small wells in the bean mixture. One at a time, crack each egg into a small bowl and slide it gently into a well. Season with ½ teaspoon salt and ¼ teaspoon pepper. Cook, covered, over medium heat, 3 to 5 minutes for slightly runny yolks.

▶ Sprinkle with the scallions and cilantro. Serve with the tortillas and sour cream.

TIP
Add the eggs to the pan just before serving or they'll quickly become overcooked.

potato, leek, and Feta tart

hands-on time: 20 minutes / total time: 1 hour, 20 minutes / serves 4

1 tablespoon olive oil

2 leeks (white and light green parts), halved lengthwise and sliced crosswise

2 small zucchini, halved lengthwise and sliced crosswise
  Kosher salt and black pepper

2 ounces Feta, crumbled (½ cup)

2 tablespoons chopped fresh dill

½ pound small red potatoes (about 2)

1 piecrust (store-bought or homemade)

▶ Heat oven to 375° F. Heat the oil in a large skillet over medium heat. Add the leeks, zucchini, ½ teaspoon salt, and ¼ teaspoon pepper and cook, tossing occasionally, until just tender, 4 to 5 minutes. Fold in the Feta and dill. Add the potatoes and toss to combine.

▶ On a piece of parchment paper, roll the piecrust to a 12-inch diameter. Slide the paper (with the piecrust) onto a baking sheet. Spoon the potato mixture onto the piecrust, leaving a 2-inch border. Fold the border of the piecrust over the potato mixture. Bake until the piecrust is golden brown (cover the edges with foil if they start to get too dark) and the potatoes are tender, 50 to 60 minutes.

TIP
For a low-fat version of this dish, use pizza dough (regular or whole wheat). There's no need to fold over the sides, and the cooking time will be slightly shorter.

dinner tonight:
desserts

classic chocolate layer cake

hands-on time: 45 minutes / total time: 2 hours (includes cooling) / serves 8

For the cake

- 1 cup (2 sticks) unsalted butter, cut into pieces, plus more for the pans
- 2 cups all-purpose flour, spooned and leveled
- 1½ cups granulated sugar
- ½ cup packed dark brown sugar
- ¾ cup unsweetened cocoa powder
- 1 teaspoon baking soda
- 1 teaspoon kosher salt
- 2 large eggs
- ½ cup sour cream
- 1 teaspoon pure vanilla extract

For the frosting

- 24 ounces semisweet chocolate, chopped
- 1½ cups (3 sticks) unsalted butter, at room temperature

▶ Make the cake: Heat oven to 350° F. Butter two 8- or 9-inch round cake pans and line each with a round of parchment paper.

▶ In a large bowl, whisk together the flour, sugars, cocoa powder, baking soda, and salt.

▶ In a small saucepan, combine the butter and 1 cup water and bring to a boil. Add to the flour mixture and, using an electric mixer, mix on low speed until combined. Beat in the eggs, one at a time, then the sour cream and vanilla.

▶ Transfer the batter to the prepared pans. Bake until a toothpick inserted in the center comes out clean, 35 to 45 minutes. Let cool in the pans for 20 minutes, then turn out onto racks to cool completely.

▶ Meanwhile, make the frosting: In a heatproof bowl set over (not in) a saucepan of simmering water, melt the chocolate, stirring often, until smooth. Let cool to room temperature (do not let solidify).

▶ Using an electric mixer, beat the butter on medium-high speed until fluffy, 1 to 2 minutes. Slowly add the chocolate and beat until smooth.

▶ Transfer one of the cooled cakes to a platter and spread with ¾ cup of the frosting. Top with the remaining cake and spread with the remaining frosting.

TIP

For flat, easy-to-layer cake rounds, turn them out of the pans onto cooling racks bottom-sides up. The domed tops will flatten as the cakes cool.

raspberry ice

hands-on time: 30 minutes / total time: 4¹/₂ hours (includes freezing) / serves 4

¹/₂ cup granulated sugar

3 cups raspberries, plus more for serving

¹/₂ cup heavy cream

▶ In a small saucepan, combine the sugar and 1 cup water. Bring to a boil, stirring to melt the sugar; let cool.

▶ In a blender, puree the raspberries with the sugar syrup. Strain into a loaf pan or shallow freezer-safe dish and freeze until firm, at least 4 hours and up to 1 day.

▶ When ready to serve, whip the cream until soft peaks form.

▶ Using a fork, scrape the surface of the frozen raspberry mixture to create icy flakes. Serve with the whipped cream and additional raspberries.

TIP
If fresh raspberries are not in season, you can use thawed frozen raspberries.

bourbon and orange pecan pie

hands-on time: 10 minutes / total time: 3 hours, 45 minutes (includes cooling) / serves 8

1 piecrust (store-bought
   or homemade), fitted into
   a 9-inch pie plate
1 cup light corn syrup
¾ cup packed light brown sugar
4 tablespoons (½ stick)
   unsalted butter, melted
3 large eggs
2 tablespoons bourbon
   (or 1 teaspoon pure
   vanilla extract)
½ teaspoon grated orange zest
½ teaspoon kosher salt
2 cups pecan halves

▶ Set an oven rack in the lowest position and heat oven to 350° F. Place the pie plate on a foil-lined baking sheet.

▶ In a large bowl, whisk together the corn syrup, sugar, butter, eggs, bourbon, orange zest, and salt. Mix in the pecans.

▶ Pour the pecan mixture into the crust and bake until the center is set, 50 to 55 minutes. Let cool to room temperature before serving.

TIP
The pie can be made up to 1 day in advance. Store, loosely covered with plastic wrap, at room temperature.

fried dough with chocolate sauce

hands-on time: 15 minutes / total time: 15 minutes / serves 4

1 pound pizza dough, thawed
  if frozen
1½ cups canola oil
  Confectioners' sugar, for
  dusting
¾ cup chocolate sauce

▶ Tear the dough into 16 pieces. Heat the oil in a large skillet over medium heat. Fry the dough until golden brown and cooked through, about 3 minutes per side; transfer to a paper towel–lined plate.

▶ Dust the fried dough with the confectioners' sugar and serve with the chocolate sauce for dipping.

TIP
To be sure the oil is hot enough for frying, flick a bit of confectioners' sugar into it—at the right temperature, the sugar will bubble. A high temperature keeps the dough from absorbing too much oil and becoming soggy.

peanut butter cup and pretzel terrine

hands-on time: 10 minutes / total time: 1 hour, 10 minutes (includes freezing) / serves 8

Nonstick cooking spray

3 pints vanilla ice cream, softened

20 miniature peanut butter cups, chopped

¾ cup broken pretzels

▶ Spray a loaf pan with the cooking spray. Line the pan with 2 crisscrossed pieces of parchment paper, spraying between the layers (to hold them in place) and leaving an overhang on each side.

▶ Press half the ice cream into the prepared pan, sprinkle with the peanut butter cups, top with the remaining ice cream, and sprinkle with the pretzels. Freeze until firm, at least 1 hour and up to 2 days.

▶ Using the parchment overhang, lift the terrine out of the pan, transfer to a platter, and slice.

TIP
To make quick, neat work of cutting this terrine and other ice cream cakes, use a warm serrated knife. Run it under hot water and dry between slices.

chocolate fudge pie

hands-on time: 20 minutes / total time: 4 hours (includes cooling) / serves 8

1 piecrust (store-bought or homemade), fitted into a 9-inch pie plate

6 ounces semisweet chocolate, chopped, plus more, shaved, for topping

½ cup (1 stick) unsalted butter

3 large eggs

⅛ teaspoon kosher salt

½ cup plus 3 tablespoons granulated sugar

1½ cups heavy cream

▶ Heat oven to 375° F. Place the pie plate on a baking sheet. Prick the crust with a fork and line with foil. Fill to the top with pie weights or dried beans. Bake until the edges are firm, 20 to 25 minutes. Remove the foil and weights and bake until just golden, 8 to 10 minutes more. Reduce oven temperature to 325° F.

▶ Meanwhile, in a large heatproof bowl set over (not in) a saucepan of simmering water, melt the chocolate and butter, stirring often, until smooth; set aside.

▶ Using an electric mixer, beat the eggs, salt, and ½ cup of the sugar on medium-high speed until fluffy, 4 to 5 minutes. Fold a third of the egg mixture into the chocolate mixture, then fold in the remainder.

▶ Pour the mixture into the crust and bake until puffed and beginning to crack, 20 to 25 minutes. Cool for 1 hour, then chill until firm, at least 2 hours.

▶ Beat the cream with the remaining 3 tablespoons of sugar on medium-high speed until soft peaks form. Spread over the pie and sprinkle with the shaved chocolate.

TIP
The pie can be prepared without the whipped cream topping and refrigerated, loosely covered with plastic wrap, for up to 2 days. Once topped with the whipped cream and shaved chocolate, it can be refrigerated, uncovered, for up to 6 hours. Bring to room temperature before serving.

poached-apricot sundaes with coconut

hands-on time: 15 minutes / total time: 35 minutes
serves 4

- ¼ cup sweetened shredded coconut
- ½ cup honey
- 2 strips lemon zest, removed with a vegetable peeler
- 4 apricots, quartered
- 1 pint vanilla ice cream

▶ Heat oven to 350° F. Spread the coconut on a rimmed baking sheet and bake, tossing occasionally, until golden, 4 to 6 minutes.

▶ In a small saucepan, combine the honey, lemon zest, and 1 cup water; bring to a boil. Add the apricots and transfer to a medium bowl. Refrigerate until cool.

▶ Divide the ice cream and apricots among bowls and top with the honey syrup (discarding the zest) and coconut.

banana-rum sundaes with toasted pecans

hands-on time: 15 minutes / total time: 15 minutes
serves 4

- ¼ cup pecans
- ½ cup heavy cream
- 1 tablespoon granulated sugar
- 1 pint vanilla ice cream
- 2 bananas, sliced
- ¼ cup dark rum

▶ Heat oven to 350° F. Spread the pecans on a rimmed baking sheet and bake, tossing occasionally, until fragrant, 6 to 8 minutes. Let cool, then roughly chop.

▶ In a large bowl, beat the cream with the sugar until soft peaks form.

▶ Divide the ice cream among bowls and top with the bananas, whipped cream, rum, and pecans.

gin-spiked blueberry sundaes

hands-on time: 10 minutes / total time: 30 minutes
serves 4

1 cup blueberries
⅓ cup gin
1 pint vanilla ice cream

▶ In a small saucepan, combine the blueberries and gin. Simmer, stirring frequently, until the berries burst and the mixture begins to thicken, 5 to 8 minutes. Transfer to a small bowl. Refrigerate until cool.

▶ Divide the ice cream among bowls and top with the blueberry sauce.

cinnamon-crisp sundaes with chocolate sauce

hands-on time: 10 minutes / total time: 10 minutes
serves 4

3 tablespoons unsalted butter
2 tablespoons granulated sugar
4 6-inch flour tortillas, cut into thin strips
½ teaspoon ground cinnamon
1 pint vanilla ice cream
½ cup chocolate sauce

▶ In a large skillet, melt the butter and sugar over medium heat. Add the tortillas and cook, tossing, until crisp, 3 to 5 minutes. Transfer to a plate and sprinkle with the cinnamon.

▶ Divide the ice cream among bowls and top with the chocolate sauce and cinnamon crisps.

peanut butter cup cookies

hands-on time: 15 minutes / total time: 40 minutes / makes 48 cookies

1½ cups all-purpose flour, spooned and leveled

 1 teaspoon baking soda

 ½ teaspoon kosher salt

 ½ cup (1 stick) unsalted butter, at room temperature

 ¾ cup packed dark brown sugar

 ½ cup granulated sugar

 1 large egg

 1 teaspoon pure vanilla extract

 1 12-ounce package miniature peanut butter cups, coarsely chopped

▶ Heat oven to 375° F. In a medium bowl, whisk together the flour, baking soda, and salt.

▶ Using an electric mixer, beat the butter and sugars on medium-high until fluffy, 2 to 3 minutes. Add the egg and vanilla and beat to combine. Reduce speed to low and gradually add the flour mixture, mixing until just combined (do not overmix). Fold in the peanut butter cups by hand.

▶ Drop tablespoonfuls of the dough onto 2 parchment-lined baking sheets, spacing them 2 inches apart. Bake until the cookies are light brown around the edges, 12 to 15 minutes. Cool slightly on the baking sheets, then transfer to wire racks to cool completely.

TIP
The cookies can be stored at room temperature in an airtight container for up to 3 days.

maple pumpkin pie

hands-on time: 10 minutes / total time: 3¹/₂ hours (includes cooling) / serves 8

1 piecrust (store-bought or homemade), fitted into a 9-inch pie plate
2 large eggs
1 15-ounce can pumpkin puree
1 cup heavy cream
¹/₂ cup pure maple syrup
³/₄ teaspoon ground cinnamon
¹/₂ teaspoon ground ginger
¹/₂ teaspoon kosher salt
¹/₈ teaspoon ground cloves

▸ Set an oven rack in the lowest position and heat oven to 350° F. Place the pie plate on a foil-lined baking sheet.

▸ In a large bowl, whisk together the eggs, pumpkin puree, cream, maple syrup, cinnamon, ginger, salt, and cloves.

▸ Pour the pumpkin mixture into the crust and bake until the center is set, 60 to 70 minutes. Let cool to room temperature before serving.

TIP
The pie can be refrigerated, loosely covered with plastic wrap, for up to 2 days. Bring to room temperature before serving.

berry and ice cream shortcakes

hands-on time: 10 minutes / total time: 10 minutes / serves 4

1 cup raspberries
1 cup blueberries
2 tablespoons granulated sugar
2 tablespoons fresh orange
   juice
4 biscuits, split
1 pint vanilla ice cream

▶ In a medium bowl, toss the raspberries and blueberries with the sugar and orange juice; let sit for 5 minutes.

▶ Serve the biscuits with the ice cream and the berry mixture.

TIP
For extra flavor, add a splash of Grand Marnier (orange-flavored liqueur) to the berry mixture.

orange–poppy seed shortbread wedges

hands-on time: 10 minutes / total time: 1 hour (includes cooling) / makes 12 wedges

1/2 cup (1 stick) cold unsalted butter, cut into pieces, plus more for the pan
1 cup all-purpose flour, spooned and leveled
1/2 cup confectioners' sugar
1/2 teaspoon kosher salt
2 teaspoons grated orange zest
2 teaspoons poppy seeds

▸ Heat oven to 350° F. Butter a 9-inch fluted removable-bottom tart pan (or a round cake pan).

▸ In a food processor, process the flour, sugar, salt, and butter until moist clumps form. Add the orange zest and poppy seeds and pulse once or twice just to combine.

▸ Press the mixture evenly into the prepared pan. Bake until lightly golden, 25 to 30 minutes.

▸ Using a serrated knife, cut the warm shortbread into 12 wedges. Let the wedges cool completely before removing them from the pan.

TIP
Zesting releases the concentrated flavors in the oils of the citrus peel. First wash the fruit, then use a Microplane or a box grater to remove the colored outer layer but not the bitter white pith.

chocolate-ricotta icebox cake

hands-on time: 15 minutes / total time: 12 hours, 15 minutes (includes chilling) / serves 8

Nonstick cooking spray
2 15-ounce containers ricotta
12 ounces semisweet chocolate, melted and cooled, plus more, shaved, for topping
½ 9-ounce package chocolate wafer cookies

▶ Spray an 8½-by-4½-inch loaf pan with the cooking spray. Line the pan with 2 crisscrossed pieces of parchment paper, spraying between the layers (to keep them in place) and leaving an overhang on each side.

▶ In a food processor, puree the ricotta with the melted chocolate until very smooth, about 1 minute.

▶ Layer a third of the ricotta mixture, then half the cookies, in the pan; repeat, then top with the remaining ricotta mixture. Refrigerate for at least 12 hours and up to 2 days.

▶ Using the parchment overhang, lift the cake out of the pan, transfer to a platter, and slice. Sprinkle with the shaved chocolate.

TIP
For a silky-smooth filling, make sure you process the ricotta and chocolate long enough and occasionally scrape down the side of the food-processor bowl.

1

2

3

4

easy yellow cupcakes with cream cheese frosting

hands-on time: 15 minutes / total time: 1½ hours (includes cooling) / makes 12 cupcakes

For the cupcakes

1¾ cups all-purpose flour, spooned and leveled

¾ cup granulated sugar

2 teaspoons baking powder

½ teaspoon baking soda

¼ teaspoon kosher salt

¾ cup plain low-fat yogurt

½ cup (1 stick) unsalted butter, melted and cooled

2 large eggs

1 teaspoon pure vanilla extract

For the frosting

1 8-ounce bar cream cheese, at room temperature

½ cup (1 stick) unsalted butter, at room temperature

1 teaspoon pure vanilla extract

3½ cups confectioners' sugar

▶ Make the cupcakes: Heat oven to 375° F. Line a 12-cup muffin tin with paper liners. In a medium bowl, whisk together the flour, sugar, baking powder, baking soda, and salt.

▶ In a large bowl, whisk together the yogurt, butter, eggs, and vanilla. Add the flour mixture and mix until just incorporated (do not overmix).

▶ Divide the batter evenly among the muffin cups. Bake until golden brown and a toothpick inserted in the center of a cupcake comes out clean, 18 to 20 minutes. Transfer the cupcakes to a wire rack to cool completely.

▶ Meanwhile, make the frosting: Using an electric mixer, beat the cream cheese, butter, and vanilla on medium-high speed until smooth, 2 to 3 minutes. Add the sugar and beat until fluffy.

▶ Frost the cooled cupcakes and decorate as desired. For the versions shown here, see Top These! (right).

TOP THESE!

1. pb & j
Mix ⅓ cup **creamy peanut butter** into frosting. Frost cupcakes. Dividing evenly, top with ¼ cup **raspberry jam** and ¼ cup **chopped roasted peanuts.**

2. strawberry hearts
Frost cupcakes. Top with 12 hearts cut from **strawberry fruit leather** with kitchen shears.

3. lemon curd
Mix ¼ cup **lemon curd** into frosting. Cut a cone-shaped piece from the top of each cupcake. Dividing evenly, fill the cavities with ¼ cup **lemon curd**; replace cut-out pieces. Frost cupcakes. Top each with half a **lemon-slice candy.**

4. triple chocolate
Mix 4 ounces **melted, cooled semisweet chocolate** into frosting. Frost cupcakes. Dividing evenly, sprinkle with 1 cup **chopped malted milk balls** and ¾ cup **chopped brownies.**

caramel-almond ice cream torte

hands-on time: 15 minutes / total time: 1 hour, 20 minutes (includes freezing) / serves 12

½ cup sliced almonds
½ gallon (4 pints) vanilla ice cream, softened
1 cup caramel sauce (slightly warmed, if thick)

▶ Heat oven to 350° F. Spread the almonds on a rimmed baking sheet and toast, tossing occasionally, until golden, 4 to 6 minutes; let cool.

▶ Press the ice cream into a 9-inch springform pan. Freeze until slightly firm, 10 to 15 minutes.

▶ Top the ice cream with the caramel sauce and almonds and freeze until firm, at least 1 hour and up to 2 days. To serve, remove the torte from the pan and cut it into wedges.

TIP
No time to let your ice cream soften at room temperature? Microwave it in its cardboard container (top removed) on high in 10-second intervals until it reaches the desired consistency.

meat cooking temperatures

The safest, most accurate way to tell when meats are done is to use an instant-read thermometer. In the following guidelines, the third column lists the U.S. Department of Agriculture's recommendations for maximum food safety. The second column gives the *Real Simple* test kitchen's preferences (considered safe by many experts) for meats cooked to juicy perfection. Temperatures are in Fahrenheit.

	RS	USDA
BEEF		
Rare	115°	NA
Medium-rare	130°	145°
Medium	140°	160°
Medium-well	150°	NA
Well-done	155°	170°
Ground beef	160°	160°
LAMB		
Medium-rare	130°	145°
Medium	140°	160°
Medium-well	150°	NA
Well-done	155°	170°
Ground lamb	160°	160°
POULTRY		
White meat	160°	165°
Dark meat	165°	165°
Ground poultry	165°	165°
PORK		
Medium	145°	160°
Well-done	160°	160°
Ground pork	160°	160°

baking-pan substitutions

When you don't have the pan that a recipe calls for, often others will do just as well. (Keep in mind that the baking time will be shorter if the pan is smaller than—or if the batter is shallower in—the pan specified in the recipe.)

pan size	capacity	substitutions
8" x 2" round	6 cups	8" x 8" x 1½" square 11" x 7" x 2" rectangle 12-cupcake tin
9" x 2" round	8 cups	8" x 8" x 2" square 11" x 7" x 2" rectangle Two 12-cupcake tins
8" x 8" x 2" square	8¾ cups	9" x 2" round Two 8½" x 4½" x 2½" loaf pans Two 12-cupcake tins
9" x 13" x 2" rectangle	16 cups	Two 9" x 2" rounds Two 8" x 8" x 2" squares Four 12-cupcake tins
11" x 7" x 2" rectangle	8 cups	9" x 2" round 8" x 8" x 2" square Two 12-cupcake tins
8½" x 4½" x 2½" loaf pan	6 cups	9" x 2" round 8" x 8" x 2" square 11" x 7" x 2" rectangle 12-cupcake tin
12-cupcake tin	6 cups	9" x 2" round 8" x 8" x 2" square 11" x 7" x 2" rectangle

measuring cheat sheet

pinch/dash	=	$1/16$ teaspoon				
1 teaspoon					=	5 ml
$1/2$ tablespoon	=	$1^1/2$ teaspoons	=	$1/4$ fl oz	=	7.5 ml
1 tablespoon	=	3 teaspoons	=	$1/2$ fl oz	=	15 ml
1 jigger	=	3 tablespoons	=	$1^1/2$ fl oz	=	45 ml
$1/4$ cup	=	4 tablespoons	=	2 fl oz	=	60 ml
$1/3$ cup	=	5 tablespoons + 1 teaspoon	=	$2^1/2$ fl oz	=	75 ml
$1/2$ cup	=	8 tablespoons	=	4 fl oz	=	120 ml
$2/3$ cup	=	10 tablespoons + 2 teaspoons	=	5 fl oz	=	150 ml
$3/4$ cup	=	12 tablespoons	=	6 fl oz	=	180 ml
1 cup	=	16 tablespoons or $1/2$ pint	=	8 fl oz	=	240 ml
1 pint	=	2 cups	=	16 fl oz	=	475 ml
1 quart	=	2 pints or 4 cups	=	32 fl oz	=	945 ml
1 gallon	=	4 quarts or 16 cups	=	128 fl oz	=	3.8 liters
1 pound	=	16 ounces				

oven temperatures

Fahrenheit		Celsius
225° F	=	110° C
250° F	=	125° C
275° F	=	135° C
300° F	=	150° C
325° F	=	160° C
350° F	=	175° C
375° F	=	190° C
400° F	=	200° C
425° F	=	220° C
450° F	=	230° C
475° F	=	245° C
500° F	=	260° C

A by-the-numbers guide to
what's in every recipe.

RECIPE KEY

30 MINUTES OR LESS

♥ HEART-HEALTHY

ONE-POT MEAL

🍄 VEGETARIAN

✖ NO-COOK

👥 FAMILY-FRIENDLY

APPETIZERS

**9   spiced beef empanadas
with lime sour cream**
PER 3-PIECE SERVING: 358 calories; 21g fat
(9g saturated fat); 63mg cholesterol; 393mg
sodium; 9g protein; 33g carbohydrates;
7g sugar; 1g fiber; 1mg iron; 25mg calcium.
👥

**9   peanut chicken skewers
with chili mayonnaise**
PER 3-PIECE SERVING: 322 calories; 26g fat
(4g saturated fat); 36mg cholesterol; 344mg
sodium; 15g protein; 6g carbohydrates;
1g sugar; 1g fiber; 1mg iron; 7mg calcium.

10   double tomato crostini
PER 3-PIECE SERVING: 156 calories; 3g fat
(0g saturated fat); 1mg cholesterol; 468mg
sodium; 6g protein; 27g carbohydrates;
2g sugar; 3g fiber; 2mg iron; 33mg calcium.
🕑🍄

10   shrimp with ginger sauce
PER SERVING: 237 calories; 1g fat (0g saturated fat); 168mg cholesterol; 433mg
sodium; 18g protein; 39g carbohydrates;
36g sugar; 0g fiber; 3mg iron; 34mg calcium.
🕑👥

11   five-minute hummus
PER ¼-CUP SERVING: 187 calories; 13g fat
(2g saturated fat); 0mg cholesterol; 428mg
sodium; 5g protein; 14g carbohydrates;
1g sugar; 4g fiber; 1mg iron; 35mg calcium.
🕑🍄✖👥

11   turkey samosas
PER 2-PIECE SERVING: 390 calories; 17g fat
(7g saturated fat); 38mg cholesterol; 320mg
sodium; 14g protein; 46g carbohydrates;
18g sugar; 0g fiber; 2mg iron; 15mg calcium.

12   prosciutto-fennel crostini
PER 3-PIECE SERVING: 198 calories;
9g fat (2g saturated fat); 22mg cholesterol;
1,020mg sodium; 12g protein;
20g carbohydrates; 1g sugar; 2g fiber;
2mg iron; 30mg calcium.
🕑

---

12   radishes with creamy ricotta
PER SERVING: 141 calories; 11g fat (6g saturated fat); 32mg cholesterol; 119mg sodium;
7g protein; 3g carbohydrates; 1g sugar;
0g fiber; 0mg iron; 133mg calcium.
🕑🍄✖

13   smoked salmon pizzettes
PER PIZZETTE: 512 calories; 18g fat (6g saturated fat); 60mg cholesterol; 772mg sodium;
28g protein; 63g carbohydrates; 4g sugar;
2g fiber; 4mg iron; 33mg calcium.
🕑

13   grilled teriyaki wings
PER 2-PIECE SERVING: 214 calories; 13g fat
(4g saturated fat); 57mg cholesterol; 667mg
sodium; 19g protein; 2g carbohydrates;
2g sugar; 0g fiber; 1mg iron; 11mg calcium.
🕑👥

**14   caramelized onion tarts
with apples**
PER 3-PIECE SERVING: 320 calories; 21g fat
(6g saturated fat); 10mg cholesterol; 403mg
sodium; 5g protein; 26g carbohydrates;
6g sugar; 2g fiber; 2mg iron; 18mg calcium.
🍄👥

**14   beef skewers with
blue cheese sauce**
PER 4-PIECE SERVING: 247 calories; 20g fat
(5g saturated fat); 25mg cholesterol; 483mg
sodium; 14g protein; 4g carbohydrates;
2g sugar; 0g fiber; 1mg iron; 42mg calcium.
🕑

**15   mini grilled cheese and
chutney sandwiches**
PER 3-PIECE SERVING: 346 calories; 18g fat
(10g saturated fat); 57g cholesterol; 558mg
sodium; 14g protein; 33g carbohydrates;
12g sugar; 2g fiber; 3mg iron; 375mg calcium.
🕑🍄👥

**15   currant-glazed cocktail
meatballs**
PER SERVING: 185 calories; 7g fat (2g saturated fat); 60mg cholesterol; 215mg sodium;
12g protein; 18g carbohydrates; 13g sugar;
0g fiber; 2mg iron; 23mg calcium.

16 baked Camembert with sun-dried tomatoes

PER SERVING: 171 calories; 10g fat (5g saturated fat); 20mg cholesterol; 337mg sodium; 8g protein; 13g carbohydrates; 0g sugar; 1g fiber; 0mg iron; 113mg calcium.

16 sweet pea and ricotta crostini

PER 4-PIECE SERVING: 424 calories; 21g fat (6g saturated fat); 21mg cholesterol; 841mg sodium; 17g protein; 43g carbohydrates; 5g sugar; 5g fiber; 3mg iron; 209mg calcium.

17 mozzarella-stuffed cherry peppers

PER 3-PIECE SERVING: 67 calories; 3g fat (2g saturated fat); 10mg cholesterol; 96mg sodium; 3g protein; 6g carbohydrates; 5g sugar; 1g fiber; 1mg iron; 79mg calcium.

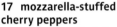

17 shrimp skewers with Feta-dill sauce

PER 2-PIECE SERVING: 308 calories; 22g fat (5g saturated fat); 185mg cholesterol; 447mg sodium; 25g protein; 2g carbohydrates; 1g sugar; 0g fiber; 3mg iron; 130mg calcium.

19 artichoke and spinach relish with walnuts

PER 3-TABLESPOON SERVING: 91 calories; 7g fat (1g saturated fat); 4mg cholesterol; 274mg sodium; 3g protein; 4g carbohydrates; 0g sugar; 2g fiber; 0mg iron; 56mg calcium.

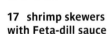

19 creamy salmon spread with horseradish

PER 3-TABLESPOON SERVING: 154 calories; 12g fat (6g saturated fat); 50mg cholesterol; 364mg sodium; 10g protein; 3g carbohydrates; 2g sugar; 0g fiber; 0mg iron; 13mg calcium.

SOUPS

23 black bean soup with smoky jalapeño salsa

PER SERVING: 262 calories; 10g fat (1g saturated fat); 0mg cholesterol; 805mg sodium; 9g protein; 33g carbohydrates; 4g sugar; 10g fiber; 3mg iron; 68mg calcium.

25 easy shrimp bisque

PER SERVING: 511 calories; 27g fat (16g saturated fat); 261mg cholesterol; 1,627mg sodium; 28g protein; 37g carbohydrates; 20g sugar; 2g fiber; 4mg iron; 100mg calcium.

27 Asian dumpling soup with shiitakes and edamame

PER SERVING: 327 calories; 9g fat (2g saturated fat); 25mg cholesterol; 889mg sodium; 29g protein; 35g carbohydrates; 8g sugar; 6g fiber; 4mg iron; 117mg calcium.

29 chicken posole

PER SERVING: 272 calories; 10g fat (2g saturated fat); 66mg cholesterol; 789mg sodium; 26g protein; 21g carbohydrates; 5g sugar; 4g fiber; 2mg iron; 22mg calcium.

31 turkey and bean chili

PER SERVING: 337 calories; 12g fat (3g saturated fat); 56mg cholesterol; 1,317mg sodium; 22g protein; 34g carbohydrates; 11g sugar; 10g fiber; 4mg iron; 134mg calcium.

33 shrimp and corn chowder with fennel

PER SERVING: 476 calories; 14g fat (7g saturated fat); 207mg cholesterol; 1,009mg sodium; 33g protein; 57g carbohydrates; 13g sugar; 7g fiber; 4mg iron; 345mg calcium.

35 French onion soup

PER SERVING: 373 calories; 18g fat (11g saturated fat); 52mg cholesterol; 580mg sodium; 15g protein; 37g carbohydrates; 10g sugar; 4g fiber; 2mg iron; 333mg calcium.

37 Tex-Mex gazpacho

PER SERVING: 221 calories; 15g fat (4g saturated fat); 13mg cholesterol; 632mg sodium; 6g protein; 19g carbohydrates; 10g sugar; 5g fiber; 2mg iron; 58mg calcium.

39 turkey, dill, and orzo soup

PER SERVING: 229 calories; 3g fat (1g saturated fat); 44mg cholesterol; 400mg sodium; 26g protein; 24g carbohydrates; 5g sugar; 2g fiber; 2mg iron; 32mg calcium.

41 smoky fish chowder

PER SERVING: 407 calories; 14g fat (4.6g saturated fat); 71mg cholesterol; 856mg sodium; 41g protein; 25g carbohydrates; 4g sugar; 3g fiber; 4mg iron; 102mg calcium.

43 kale and white bean soup

PER SERVING: 205 calories; 6g fat (2g saturated fat); 5mg cholesterol; 610mg sodium; 10g protein; 29g carbohydrates; 1g sugar; 5g fiber; 3mg iron; 225mg calcium.

SALADS

47 creamy shrimp salad with endive and cucumber

PER SERVING: 216 calories; 5g fat (2g saturated fat); 183mg cholesterol; 483mg sodium; 28g protein; 14g carbohydrates; 3g sugar; 9g fiber; 5mg iron; 247mg calcium.

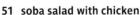

49 turkey and blue cheese salad

PER SERVING: 334 calories; 23g fat (7g saturated fat); 64mg cholesterol; 1,205mg sodium; 27g protein; 7g carbohydrates; 3g sugar; 3g fiber; 3mg iron; 228mg calcium.

51 soba salad with chicken

PER SERVING: 599 calories; 27g fat (3g saturated fat); 94mg cholesterol; 697mg sodium; 44g protein; 44g carbohydrates; 5g sugar; 4g fiber; 4mg iron; 68mg calcium.

53 minty bulgur salad with salmon and cucumbers

PER SERVING: 380 calories; 14g fat (2g saturated fat); 72mg cholesterol; 436mg sodium; 32g protein; 35g carbohydrates; 3g sugar; 8g fiber; 4mg iron; 87mg calcium.

55 romaine salad with turkey and manchego

PER SERVING: 363 calories; 25g fat (9g saturated fat); 68mg cholesterol; 1,329mg sodium; 26g protein; 13g carbohydrates; 4g sugar; 3g fiber; 2mg iron; 355mg calcium.

57 spinach, shrimp, and avocado salad

PER SERVING: 313 calories; 19g fat (3g saturated fat); 172mg cholesterol; 541mg sodium; 26g protein; 11g carbohydrates; 3g sugar; 5g fiber; 5mg iron; 133mg calcium.

58 romaine salad with tomatoes and bacon

PER SERVING: 153 calories; 13g fat (3g saturated fat); 12mg cholesterol; 251mg sodium; 6g protein; 6g carbohydrates; 3g sugar; 3g fiber; 1mg iron; 106mg calcium.

58 mesclun salad with chickpeas and dried cherries

PER SERVING: 247 calories; 11g fat (1g saturated fat); 0mg cholesterol; 326mg sodium; 6g protein; 32g carbohydrates; 14g sugar; 7g fiber; 2mg iron; 47mg calcium.

59 arugula salad with green beans and radishes

PER SERVING: 134 calories; 10g fat (2g saturated fat); 6mg cholesterol; 156mg sodium; 4g protein; 8g carbohydrates; 1g sugar; 3g fiber; 1mg iron; 152mg calcium.

59 watercress salad with beets and Feta

PER SERVING: 146 calories; 10g fat (3g saturated fat); 13mg cholesterol; 506mg sodium; 4g protein; 12g carbohydrates; 8g sugar; 2g fiber; 2mg iron; 148mg calcium.

61 Moroccan chicken salad with carrots

PER SERVING: 433 calories; 21g fat (3g saturated fat); 94mg cholesterol; 667mg sodium; 37g protein; 26g carbohydrates; 14g sugar; 5g fiber; 3mg iron; 83mg calcium.

63 grilled salmon salad with grapefruit

PER SERVING: 441 calories; 26g fat (4g saturated fat); 108mg cholesterol; 469mg sodium; 41g protein; 12g carbohydrates; 6g sugar; 5g fiber; 2mg iron; 38mg calcium.

65 Asian beef and cabbage salad

PER SERVING: 367 calories; 23g fat (5g saturated fat); 69mg cholesterol; 442mg sodium; 24g protein; 13g carbohydrates; 8g sugar; 3g fiber; 3mg iron; 78mg calcium.

67 Caesar salad with grilled chicken and garlic

PER SERVING: 481 calories; 20g fat (5g saturated fat); 123mg cholesterol; 1,624mg sodium; 52g protein; 23g carbohydrates; 2g sugar; 2g fiber; 4mg iron; 325mg calcium.

69 chopped steak salad

PER SERVING: 252 calories; 10g fat (3g saturated fat); 30mg cholesterol; 731mg sodium; 23g protein; 18g carbohydrates; 5g sugar; 4g fiber; 3mg iron; 86mg calcium.

71 Mediterranean salad with shrimp and chickpeas

PER SERVING: 473 calories; 24g fat (6g saturated fat); 191mg cholesterol; 1,065mg sodium; 33g protein; 31g carbohydrates; 6g sugar; 6g fiber; 5mg iron; 264mg calcium.

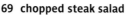

73 turkey Waldorf salad

PER SERVING: 186 calories; 11g fat (2g saturated fat); 32mg cholesterol; 330mg sodium; 13g protein; 10g carbohydrates; 6g sugar; 2g fiber; 2mg iron; 48mg calcium.

POULTRY

77 braised chicken and spring vegetables

PER SERVING: 273 calories; 13g fat (3.5g saturated fat); 100mg cholesterol; 426mg sodium; 29g protein; 9g carbohydrates; 5g sugar; 2g fiber; 2mg iron; 47mg calcium.

79 Havarti-stuffed chicken breasts with tomato salad

PER SERVING: 334 calories; 18g fat (9g saturated fat); 119mg cholesterol; 474mg sodium; 39g protein; 0g carbohydrates; 0g sugar; 0g fiber; 1mg iron; 220mg calcium.

81 crispy turkey cutlets with green bean salad

PER SERVING: 448 calories; 22g fat (3g saturated fat); 151mg cholesterol; 873mg sodium; 37g protein; 28g carbohydrates; 3g sugar; 4g fiber; 4mg iron; 79mg calcium.

83 Thai red curry chicken

PER SERVING: 700 calories; 38g fat (22g saturated fat); 94mg cholesterol; 519mg sodium; 41g protein; 49g carbohydrates; 2g sugar; 4g fiber; 7mg iron; 66mg calcium.

85 roasted chicken with tomatoes and olives

PER SERVING: 595 calories; 37g fat (8g saturated fat); 142mg cholesterol; 966mg sodium; 47g protein; 15g carbohydrates; 5g sugar; 3g fiber; 4mg iron; 88mg calcium.

87 chicken, ham, and Swiss roulades
PER SERVING: 524 calories; 31g fat (10g saturated fat); 147mg cholesterol; 1,132mg sodium; 53g protein; 7g carbohydrates; 4g sugar; 3g fiber; 3mg iron; 421mg calcium.

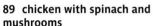

89 chicken with spinach and mushrooms
PER SERVING: 295 calories; 11g fat (2g saturated fat); 94mg cholesterol; 615mg sodium; 38g protein; 7g carbohydrates; 3g sugar; 2g fiber; 3mg iron; 84mg calcium.

91 roasted chicken with carrots and potatoes
PER SERVING: 598 calories; 31g fat (10g saturated fat); 134mg cholesterol; 672mg sodium; 41g protein; 38g carbohydrates; 7g sugar; 6g fiber; 4mg iron; 81mg calcium.

93 turkey Reubens
PER SERVING: 642 calories; 32g fat (12g saturated fat); 83mg cholesterol; 1,912mg sodium; 36g protein; 51g carbohydrates; 5g sugar; 7g fiber; 3mg iron; 470mg calcium.

95 chicken and pepper stew with olives
PER SERVING: 563 calories; 20g fat (4.5g saturated fat); 100mg cholesterol; 713mg sodium; 34g protein; 61g carbohydrates; 9g sugar; 4g fiber; 5mg iron; 66mg calcium.

97 grilled lemon chicken with cabbage and corn slaw
PER SERVING: 326 calories; 12g fat (2g saturated fat); 94mg cholesterol; 602mg sodium; 37g protein; 17g carbohydrates; 8g sugar; 4g fiber; 2mg iron; 53mg calcium.

99 chicken with creamy mushrooms
PER SERVING: 454 calories; 29g fat (14g saturated fat); 153mg cholesterol; 578mg sodium; 43g protein; 5g carbohydrates; 2g sugar; 1g fiber; 2mg iron; 113mg calcium.

101 spicy orange-glazed drumsticks with green beans
PER SERVING: 542 calories; 16g fat (5g saturated fat); 102mg cholesterol; 974mg sodium; 37g protein; 64g carbohydrates; 19g sugar; 7g fiber; 4mg iron; 314mg calcium.

103 chicken and chorizo tostadas
PER SERVING: 608 calories; 40g fat (19g saturated fat); 141mg cholesterol; 1,191mg sodium; 41g protein; 18g carbohydrates; 1g sugar; 1g fiber; 3mg iron; 470mg calcium.

105 chicken with shallots and mashed sweet potatoes
PER SERVING: 424 calories; 18g fat (3g saturated fat); 94mg cholesterol; 718mg sodium; 37g protein; 29g carbohydrates; 9g sugar; 4g fiber; 3mg iron; 57mg calcium.

107 baked chicken Parmesan
PER SERVING: 856 calories; 48g fat (20g saturated fat); 280mg cholesterol; 1,655mg sodium; 64g protein; 38g carbohydrates; 16g sugar; 2g fiber; 4mg iron; 704mg calcium.

109 spiced chicken with couscous salad
PER SERVING: 433 calories; 15g fat (3g saturated fat); 94mg cholesterol; 575mg sodium; 41g protein; 34g carbohydrates; 4g sugar; 4g fiber; 3mg iron; 71mg calcium.

111 chicken with fennel-orange salad
PER SERVING: 357 calories; 18g fat (3g saturated fat); 94mg cholesterol; 361mg sodium; 36g protein; 13g carbohydrates; 6g sugar; 4g fiber; 3mg iron; 93mg calcium.

113 chicken with broccoli rabe, apricots, and pine nuts
PER SERVING: 324 calories; 13g fat (2g saturated fat); 94mg cholesterol; 477mg sodium; 39g protein; 13g carbohydrates; 2g sugar; 1g fiber; 3mg iron; 79mg calcium.

115 crispy herbed chicken strips
PER SERVING: 597 calories; 31g fat (5g saturated fat); 148mg cholesterol; 668mg sodium; 41g protein; 37g carbohydrates; 6g sugar; 2g fiber; 3mg iron; 58mg calcium.

117 turkey hash with fried eggs
PER SERVING: 368 calories; 22g fat (5g saturated fat); 447mg cholesterol; 412mg sodium; 25g protein; 19g carbohydrates; 4g sugar; 3g fiber; 3mg iron; 82mg calcium.

119 chicken and prosciutto club sandwiches
PER SERVING: 472 calories; 27g fat (5g saturated fat); 76mg cholesterol; 1,434mg sodium; 30g protein; 26g carbohydrates; 3g sugar; 1g fiber; 3mg iron; 93mg calcium.

BEEF & LAMB

123 grilled beef and pepper fajitas
PER SERVING: 547 calories; 28g fat (9g saturated fat); 60mg cholesterol; 834mg sodium; 32g protein; 42g carbohydrates; 5g sugar; 6g fiber; 4mg iron; 135mg calcium.

125 Gouda cheeseburgers with fennel-onion relish
PER SERVING: 876 calories; 43g fat (15g saturated fat); 160mg cholesterol; 1,424mg sodium; 55g protein; 67g carbohydrates; 16g sugar; 7mg iron; 354mg calcium.

127 lamb chops with curried rice and cherries
PER SERVING: 415 calories; 10g fat (3g saturated fat); 87mg cholesterol; 318mg sodium; 31g protein; 52g carbohydrates; 5g sugar; 3g fiber; 4mg iron; 34mg calcium.

129 classic beef stew
PER SERVING: 495 calories; 16g fat (5g saturated fat); 119mg cholesterol; 591mg sodium; 62g protein; 22g carbohydrates; 10g sugar; 5g fiber; 6mg iron; 89mg calcium.

131 steak with potato-parsnip mash
PER SERVING: 473 calories; 24g fat (10g saturated fat); 125mg cholesterol; 610mg sodium; 37g protein; 25g carbohydrates; 2g sugar; 2g fiber; 3mg iron; 74mg calcium.

133 broccoli rabe and beef flat bread
PER SERVING: 645 calories; 30g fat (11g saturated fat); 79mg cholesterol; 863mg sodium; 35g protein; 63g carbohydrates; 3g sugar; 3g fiber; 5mg iron; 314mg calcium.

135 slow-cooker Cuban braised beef and peppers
PER SERVING: 556 calories; 17g fat (4.7g saturated fat); 56mg cholesterol; 883mg sodium; 44g protein; 55g carbohydrates; 7g sugar; 7g fiber; 6mg iron; 93mg calcium.

137 grilled steak, plums, and bok choy
PER SERVING: 335 calories; 15g fat (5g saturated fat); 60mg cholesterol; 1,327mg sodium; 39g protein; 10g carbohydrates; 9g sugar; 2g fiber; 3mg iron; 38mg calcium.

139 spiced lamb chops with chickpea and carrot sauté
PER SERVING: 311 calories; 13g fat (4g saturated fat); 87mg cholesterol; 720mg sodium; 32g protein; 15g carbohydrates; 2g sugar; 4g fiber; 3mg iron; 58mg calcium.

141 beef and sweet potato turnovers
PER SERVING: 293 calories; 18g fat (7g saturated fat); 49mg cholesterol; 498mg sodium; 17g protein; 15g carbohydrates; 2g sugar; 2g fiber; 2mg iron; 125mg calcium.

143 Cajun skirt steak with creamed corn
PER SERVING: 663 calories; 40g fat (18g saturated fat); 139mg cholesterol; 930mg sodium; 42g protein; 38g carbohydrates; 8g sugar; 6g fiber; 5mg iron; 91mg calcium.

145 spicy beef kebabs with minted watermelon salad
PER SERVING: 361 calories; 14g fat (5g saturated fat); 111mg cholesterol; 458mg sodium; 38g protein; 24g carbohydrates; 19g sugar; 2g fiber; 5mg iron; 45mg calcium.

147 lamb with golden Israeli couscous
PER SERVING: 650 calories; 32g fat (11g saturated fat); 131mg cholesterol; 868mg sodium; 40g protein; 50g carbohydrates; 11g sugar; 5g fiber; 6mg iron; 62mg calcium.

149 steak with potato salad and blue cheese vinaigrette
PER SERVING: 390 calories; 14g fat (6g saturated fat); 79mg cholesterol; 898mg sodium; 43g protein; 21g carbohydrates; 1g sugar; 3g fiber; 5mg iron; 83mg calcium.

151 sweet and spicy beef stir-fry
PER SERVING: 462 calories; 11g fat (3g saturated fat); 40mg cholesterol; 638mg sodium; 33g protein; 59g carbohydrates; 23g sugar; 4g fiber; 5mg iron; 66mg calcium.

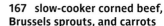

153 deep-dish cheeseburger pizza
PER SERVING: 606 calories; 28g fat (10g saturated fat); 64mg cholesterol; 788mg sodium; 29g protein; 64g carbohydrates; 8g sugar; 3g fiber; 5mg iron; 223mg calcium.

155 Tuscan lamb with garlicky tomato sauce and polenta
PER SERVING: 385 calories; 13g fat (5g saturated fat); 95mg cholesterol; 1,143mg sodium; 32g protein; 28g carbohydrates; 5g sugar; 3g fiber; 4mg iron; 25mg calcium.

157 steak sandwiches with Brie
PER SERVING: 552 calories; 24g fat (12g saturated fat); 77mg cholesterol; 1,176mg sodium; 34g protein; 49g carbohydrates; 3g sugar; 2g fiber; 4mg iron; 160mg calcium.

159 steak with crispy potatoes and pistachio pesto
PER SERVING: 625 calories; 36g fat (7g saturated fat); 74mg cholesterol; 598mg sodium; 42g protein; 36g carbohydrates; 4g sugar; 4g fiber; 5mg iron; 114mg calcium.

161 balsamic-glazed lamb meat loaf
PER SERVING: 504 calories; 35g fat (13g saturated fat); 136mg cholesterol; 842mg sodium; 24g protein; 21g carbohydrates; 3g sugar; 4g fiber; 4mg iron; 82mg calcium.

163 cottage pies
PER SERVING: 469 calories; 20g fat (8g saturated fat); 87mg cholesterol; 999mg sodium; 29g protein; 44g carbohydrates; 9g sugar; 4g fiber; 5mg iron; 72mg calcium.

165 quick beef tacos
PER SERVING: 697 calories; 48g fat (13g saturated fat); 121mg cholesterol; 1,326mg sodium; 38g protein; 30g carbohydrates; 4g sugar; 8g fiber; 4mg iron; 97mg calcium.

167 slow-cooker corned beef, Brussels sprouts, and carrots
PER SERVING: 512 calories; 31g fat (12g saturated fat); 152mg cholesterol; 1,729mg sodium; 30g protein; 22g carbohydrates; 8g sugar; 6g fiber; 4mg iron; 99mg calcium.

169 seared lamb chops with minted spaghetti squash
PER SERVING: 325 calories; 18g fat (4g saturated fat); 68mg cholesterol; 597mg sodium; 23g protein; 21g carbohydrates; 8g sugar; 5g fiber; 3mg iron; 95mg calcium.

PORK

173 roasted pork chops and peaches
PER SERVING: 532 calories; 14g fat (4g saturated fat); 92mg cholesterol; 435mg sodium; 44g protein; 59g carbohydrates; 6g sugar; 4g fiber; 3mg iron; 72mg calcium.

175 brown sugar–glazed pork with grilled corn
PER SERVING: 342 calories; 12g fat (5g saturated fat); 108mg cholesterol; 670mg sodium; 33g protein; 28g carbohydrates; 12g sugar; 3g fiber; 3mg iron; 42mg calcium.

177 sausage and white bean casserole
PER SERVING: 510 calories; 29g fat (9g saturated fat); 62mg cholesterol; 1,802mg sodium; 26g protein; 36g carbohydrates; 4g sugar; 10g fiber; 8mg iron; 240mg calcium.

179 paprika-spiced pork chops with spinach sauté
PER SERVING: 345 calories; 16g fat (5g saturated fat); 91mg cholesterol; 472mg sodium; 39g protein; 12g carbohydrates; 6g sugar; 3g fiber; 4mg iron; 116mg calcium.

181 ham, Gruyère, and shallot pizza
PER SERVING: 305 calories; 10g fat (3g saturated fat); 24mg cholesterol; 865mg sodium; 16g protein; 38g carbohydrates; 3g sugar; 2g fiber; 3mg iron; 111mg calcium.

183 pork chops with garlicky broccoli
PER SERVING: 474 calories; 17g fat (4g saturated fat); 61mg cholesterol; 506mg sodium; 30g protein; 50g carbohydrates; 1g sugar; 3g fiber; 3mg iron; 97mg calcium.

185 jalapeño pork stew with pickled onions
PER SERVING: 917 calories; 54g fat (18g saturated fat); 240mg cholesterol; 741mg sodium; 66g protein; 38g carbohydrates; 5g sugar; 4g fiber; 6mg iron; 95mg calcium.

187 apricot-glazed ham with potatoes and asparagus
PER SERVING: 443 calories; 19g fat (4g saturated fat); 109mg cholesterol; 2,042mg sodium; 41g protein; 28g carbohydrates; 9g sugar; 3g fiber; 4mg iron; 37mg calcium.

189 spiced pork chops with red cabbage
PER SERVING: 469 calories; 23g fat (6g saturated fat); 102mg cholesterol; 716mg sodium; 41g protein; 25g carbohydrates; 16g sugar; 4g fiber; 3mg iron; 109mg calcium.

191 sausage and broccoli calzones
PER SERVING: 879 calories; 50g fat (19g saturated fat); 99mg cholesterol; 1,888mg sodium; 42g protein; 69g carbohydrates; 10g sugar; 3g fiber; 5mg iron; 470mg calcium.

193 meatballs with pine nuts and raisins
PER SERVING: 509 calories; 39g fat (12g saturated fat); 102mg cholesterol; 1,169mg sodium; 29g protein; 11g carbohydrates; 3g sugar; 5g fiber; 7mg iron; 149mg calcium.

195 pork chops with mustard sauce and tarragon
PER SERVING: 364 calories; 19g fat (6g saturated fat); 108mg cholesterol; 357mg sodium; 37g protein; 6g carbohydrates; 1g sugar; 2g fiber; 2mg iron; 75mg calcium.

197 tapas plate with marinated chickpeas
PER SERVING: 706 calories; 38g fat (17g saturated fat); 82mg cholesterol; 2,083mg sodium; 33g protein; 59g carbohydrates; 17g sugar; 8g fiber; 4mg iron; 717mg calcium.

199 grilled pork chops and cherry tomatoes
PER SERVING: 427 calories; 23g fat (11g saturated fat); 145mg cholesterol; 577mg sodium; 45g protein; 10g carbohydrates; 6g sugar; 3g fiber; 2mg iron; 73mg calcium.

201 roasted pork with Brussels sprouts and apricots
PER SERVING: 313 calories; 14g fat (3g saturated fat); 84mg cholesterol; 560mg sodium; 34g protein; 13g carbohydrates; 6g sugar; 4g fiber; 3mg iron; 56mg calcium.

203 pork chops with butter bean salad
PER SERVING: 434 calories; 24g fat (6g saturated fat); 97mg cholesterol; 1,104mg sodium; 42g protein; 16g carbohydrates; 1g sugar; 5g fiber; 5mg iron; 163mg calcium.

205 gingery pork and cucumber pitas
PER SERVING: 516 calories; 23g fat (7g saturated fat); 80mg cholesterol; 766mg sodium; 29g protein; 49g carbohydrates; 10g sugar; 3g fiber; 3mg iron; 100mg calcium.

207 cranberry-stuffed pork chops with roasted carrots
PER SERVING: 518 calories; 22g fat (6g saturated fat); 115mg cholesterol; 670mg sodium; 44g protein; 35g carbohydrates; 26g sugar; 5g fiber; 2mg iron; 99mg calcium.

209 sausages with smashed potatoes and cornichons
PER SERVING: 688 calories; 47g fat (14g saturated fat); 76mg cholesterol; 2,111mg sodium; 29g protein; 37g carbohydrates; 6g sugar; 4g fiber; 4mg iron; 59mg calcium.

211 fennel-crusted pork with roasted root vegetables
PER SERVING: 400 calories; 15g fat (3g saturated fat); 92mg cholesterol; 620mg sodium; 32g protein; 35g carbohydrates; 17g sugar; 8g fiber; 3mg iron; 106mg calcium.

213 slow-cooker sweet and spicy Asian pork shoulder
PER SERVING: 780 calories; 24g fat (8g saturated fat); 193mg cholesterol; 1,498mg sodium; 64g protein; 75g carbohydrates; 29g sugar; 3g fiber; 8mg iron; 332mg calcium.

SEAFOOD

217 salmon with brown butter, almonds, and green beans
PER SERVING: 396 calories; 25g fat (9g saturated fat); 120mg cholesterol; 506mg sodium; 36g protein; 9g carbohydrates; 2g sugar; 4g fiber; 3mg iron; 77mg calcium.

219 creamy rice with roasted shrimp and tomatoes
PER SERVING: 412 calories; 10g fat (1g saturated fat); 172mg cholesterol; 658mg sodium; 29g protein; 50g carbohydrates; 5g sugar; 5g fiber; 4mg iron; 101mg calcium.

221 ginger-glazed cod with sautéed summer squash
PER SERVING: 253 calories; 10g fat (1g saturated fat); 65mg cholesterol; 556mg sodium; 29g protein; 13g carbohydrates; 10g sugar; 2g fiber; 1mg iron; 52mg calcium.

223 salmon kebabs with cilantro sauce
PER SERVING: 479 calories; 28g fat (4g saturated fat); 90mg cholesterol; 437mg sodium; 37g protein; 20g carbohydrates; 3g sugar; 1g fiber; 3mg iron; 42mg calcium.

225 creamy shrimp with corn and poblanos
PER SERVING: 590 calories; 23g fat (11g saturated fat); 320mg cholesterol; 549mg sodium; 41g protein; 52g carbohydrates; 1g sugar; 3g fiber; 6mg iron; 132mg calcium.

227 tilapia with watercress and mango salad
PER SERVING: 333 calories; 18g fat (3g saturated fat); 71mg cholesterol; 457mg sodium; 30g protein; 14g carbohydrates; 11g sugar; 2g fiber; 1mg iron; 85mg calcium.

229 Dijon salmon cakes with couscous
PER SERVING: 552 calories; 20g fat (3g saturated fat); 72mg cholesterol; 721mg sodium; 36g protein; 58g carbohydrates; 3g sugar; 3g fiber; 3mg iron; 52mg calcium.

231 halibut with tomatoes and capers
PER SERVING: 326 calories; 10g fat (1g saturated fat); 70mg cholesterol; 614mg sodium; 47g protein; 11g carbohydrates; 7g sugar; 2g fiber; 3mg iron; 132mg calcium.

233 shrimp potpie with fennel
PER SERVING: 559 calories; 30g fat (7g saturated fat); 179mg cholesterol; 1,113mg sodium; 31g protein; 39g carbohydrates; 6g sugar; 4g fiber; 6mg iron; 196mg calcium.

235 curry-roasted salmon with tomatoes
PER SERVING: 463 calories; 14g fat (2g saturated fat); 90mg cholesterol; 437mg sodium; 37g protein; 44g carbohydrates; 2g sugar; 2g fiber; 4mg iron; 51mg calcium.

237 parchment-baked halibut with spinach and basil
PER SERVING: 320 calories; 9g fat (1g saturated fat); 70mg cholesterol; 548mg sodium; 50g protein; 10g carbohydrates; 4g sugar; 5g fiber; 5mg iron; 286mg calcium.

239 seared scallops with snow peas and orange
PER SERVING: 343 calories; 7g fat (1g saturated fat); 43mg cholesterol; 455mg sodium; 27g protein; 45g carbohydrates; 4g sugar; 4g fiber; 4mg iron; 78mg calcium.

241 roasted salmon and peppers with caper vinaigrette
PER SERVING: 505 calories; 18g fat (3g saturated fat); 90mg cholesterol; 530mg sodium; 37g protein; 47g carbohydrates; 2g sugar; 3g fiber; 4mg iron; 72mg calcium.

243 mussels with pesto and garlic oven fries
PER SERVING: 631 calories; 26g fat (6g saturated fat); 74mg cholesterol; 1,261mg sodium; 38g protein; 54g carbohydrates; 2g sugar; 4g fiber; 12mg iron; 319mg calcium.

245 shrimp and bacon with Cheddar grits
PER SERVING: 447 calories; 17g fat (8g saturated fat); 211mg cholesterol; 1,067mg sodium; 36g protein; 36g carbohydrates; 1g sugar; 1g fiber; 5mg iron; 280mg calcium.

247 honey-soy glazed salmon with spinach and peppers
PER SERVING: 322 calories; 15g fat (2g saturated fat); 90mg cholesterol; 725mg sodium; 36g protein; 10g carbohydrates; 6g sugar; 3g fiber; 4mg iron; 119mg calcium.

249 curried shrimp rolls
PER SERVING: 312 calories; 14g fat (2g saturated fat); 173mg cholesterol; 612mg sodium; 22g protein; 23g carbohydrates; 3g sugar; 1g fiber; 4mg iron; 112mg calcium.

251 ancho-rubbed salmon with summer squash
PER SERVING: 315 calories; 17g fat (3g saturated fat); 90mg cholesterol; 564mg sodium; 33g protein; 6g carbohydrates; 5g sugar; 1g fiber; 2mg iron; 37mg calcium.

253 tilapia with peppers and olives
PER SERVING: 276 calories; 13g fat (3g saturated fat); 73mg cholesterol; 540mg sodium; 35g protein; 8g carbohydrates; 4g sugar; 3g fiber; 2mg iron; 48mg calcium.

255 grilled shrimp with lemony potato salad
PER SERVING: 276 calories; 11g fat (3g saturated fat); 139mg cholesterol; 1,371mg sodium; 21g protein; 23g carbohydrates; 3g sugar; 3g fiber; 4mg iron; 92mg calcium.

257 salmon, black bean, and corn tostadas
PER SERVING: 429 calories; 17g fat (3g saturated fat); 90mg cholesterol; 653mg sodium; 38g protein; 31g carbohydrates; 3g sugar; 6g fiber; 3mg iron; 69mg calcium.

259 hoisin-glazed shrimp skewers with cucumber salad
PER SERVING: 240 calories; 10g fat (1g saturated fat); 173mg cholesterol; 552mg sodium; 25g protein; 12g carbohydrates; 6g sugar; 1g fiber; 3mg iron; 87mg calcium.

261 salmon with warm lentil salad
PER SERVING: 466 calories; 19g fat (3g saturated fat); 90mg cholesterol; 467mg sodium; 43g protein; 30g carbohydrates; 2g sugar; 8g fiber; 5mg iron; 86mg calcium.

PASTA

265 spaghetti with zucchini, walnuts, and raisins
PER SERVING: 641 calories; 23g fat (4g saturated fat); 5mg cholesterol; 387mg sodium; 20g protein; 94g carbohydrates; 20g sugar; 8g fiber; 4mg iron; 171mg calcium.

267 gnocchi with roasted cauliflower
PER SERVING: 331 calories; 13g fat (2g saturated fat); 5mg cholesterol; 771mg sodium; 10g protein; 46g carbohydrates; 3g sugar; 7g fiber; 2mg iron; 149mg calcium.

269 pasta with chicken sausage and broccoli
PER SERVING: 512 calories; 11g fat (3g saturated fat); 40mg cholesterol; 431mg sodium; 27g protein; 80g carbohydrates; 7g sugar; 8g fiber; 5mg iron; 204mg calcium.

271 spinach and ricotta–stuffed shells
PER SERVING: 794 calories; 47g fat (24g saturated fat); 141mg cholesterol; 1,390mg sodium; 44g protein; 49g carbohydrates; 9g sugar; 5g fiber; 3mg iron; 798mg calcium.

273 spaghetti with shrimp, Feta, and dill
PER SERVING: 675 calories; 27g fat (7g saturated fat); 197mg cholesterol; 844mg sodium; 39g protein; 67g carbohydrates; 3g sugar; 4g fiber; 6mg iron; 215mg calcium.

274 ravioli with peas and crispy bacon
PER SERVING: 590 calories; 29g fat (13g saturated fat); 91mg cholesterol; 1,127mg sodium; 23g protein; 59g carbohydrates; 6g sugar; 7g fiber; 3mg iron; 197mg calcium.
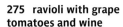

274 ravioli with brown butter and sage
PER SERVING: 568 calories; 34g fat (18g saturated fat); 110mg cholesterol; 837mg sodium; 17g protein; 50g carbohydrates; 4g sugar; 4g fiber; 2mg iron; 185mg calcium.

275 ravioli with grape tomatoes and wine
PER SERVING: 510 calories; 23g fat (11g saturated fat); 80mg cholesterol; 842mg sodium; 16g protein; 55g carbohydrates; 6g sugar; 4g fiber; 3mg iron; 179mg calcium.

275 creamy ravioli and pesto gratin
PER SERVING: 669 calories; 42g fat (23g saturated fat); 156mg cholesterol; 861mg sodium; 22g protein; 51g carbohydrates; 3g sugar; 4g fiber; 2mg iron; 411mg calcium.

277 pasta with Brie, mushrooms, and arugula
PER SERVING: 578 calories; 21g fat (11g saturated fat); 57mg cholesterol; 615mg sodium; 26g protein; 70g carbohydrates; 8g sugar; 3g fiber; 4mg iron; 163mg calcium.

279 spaghetti with sweet potatoes and ricotta
PER SERVING: 551 calories; 13g fat (4g saturated fat); 16mg cholesterol; 566mg sodium; 20g protein; 87g carbohydrates; 8g sugar; 7g fiber; 4mg iron; 177mg calcium.

281 pappardelle with spicy meat sauce

PER SERVING: 543 calories; 15g fat (5g saturated fat); 63mg cholesterol; 659mg sodium; 36g protein; 64g carbohydrates; 0g sugar; 7g fiber; 7mg iron; 290mg calcium.

283 creamy pecorino pasta with radicchio salad

PER SERVING: 594 calories; 28g fat (17g saturated fat); 92mg cholesterol; 985mg sodium; 21g protein; 66g carbohydrates; 3g sugar; 5g fiber; 4mg iron; 292mg calcium.

285 rigatoni peperonata

PER SERVING: 563 calories; 25g fat (3g saturated fat); 0mg cholesterol; 523mg sodium; 13g protein; 74g carbohydrates; 7g sugar; 4g fiber; 3mg iron; 23mg calcium.

287 pasta with bacon and cauliflower

PER SERVING: 489 calories; 12g fat (4.7g saturated fat); 26mg cholesterol; 737mg sodium; 26g protein; 68g carbohydrates; 3g sugar; 5g fiber; 3mg iron; 347mg calcium.

289 lasagna with broccoli and three cheeses

PER SERVING: 833 calories; 56g fat (27g saturated fat); 155mg cholesterol; 1,502mg sodium; 39g protein; 41g carbohydrates; 7g sugar; 7g fiber; 2mg iron; 786mg calcium.

291 fettuccine with lima beans, peas, and leeks

PER SERVING: 684 calories; 27g fat (13g saturated fat); 66mg cholesterol; 317mg sodium; 22g protein; 90g carbohydrates; 8g sugar; 9g fiber; 6mg iron; 202mg calcium.

VEGETARIAN

295 eggplant lasagna with fresh basil

PER SERVING: 378 calories; 26g fat (9g saturated fat); 91mg cholesterol; 782mg sodium; 15g protein; 27g carbohydrates; 11g sugar; 14g fiber; 2mg iron; 245mg calcium.

297 tofu tacos with spinach, corn, and goat cheese

PER SERVING: 355 calories; 14g fat (3g saturated fat); 7mg cholesterol; 646mg sodium; 18g protein; 46g carbohydrates; 4g sugar; 7g fiber; 4mg iron; 289mg calcium.

299 poached eggs with mushrooms and tomatoes

PER SERVING: 333 calories; 16g fat (4g saturated fat); 423mg cholesterol; 831mg sodium; 19g protein; 28g carbohydrates; 9g sugar; 3g fiber; 4mg iron; 111mg calcium.

301 creamy barley with tomatoes and greens

PER SERVING: 605 calories; 16g fat (6g saturated fat); 24mg cholesterol; 917mg sodium; 23g protein; 91g carbohydrates; 7g sugar; 21g fiber; 5mg iron; 380mg calcium.

303 pierogi with sautéed red cabbage

PER SERVING: 297 calories; 9g fat (1g saturated fat); 5mg cholesterol; 682mg sodium; 7g protein; 50g carbohydrates; 10g sugar; 5g fiber; 3mg iron; 73mg calcium.

304 spicy three-pepper pizza

PER SERVING: 626 calories; 28g fat (12g saturated fat); 59mg cholesterol; 1,063mg sodium; 28g protein; 70g carbohydrates; 8g sugar; 3g fiber; 4mg iron; 561mg calcium.

304 squash-Cheddar flat bread

PER SERVING: 605 calories; 27g fat (10g saturated fat); 46mg cholesterol; 1,039mg sodium; 22g protein; 70g carbohydrates; 6g sugar; 5g fiber; 5mg iron; 366mg calcium.

305 tomato-olive pizza

PER SERVING: 379 calories; 11g fat (1g saturated fat); 0mg cholesterol; 642mg sodium; 12g protein; 59g carbohydrates; 5g sugar; 4g fiber; 4mg iron; 19mg calcium.

305 potato-rosemary flat bread

PER SERVING: 459 calories; 16g fat (3g saturated fat); 0mg cholesterol; 595mg sodium; 12g protein; 70g carbohydrates; 2g sugar; 3g fiber; 4mg iron; 7mg calcium.

307 stir-fried rice noodles with tofu and vegetables

PER SERVING: 512 calories; 15g fat (1g saturated fat); 0mg cholesterol; 529mg sodium; 19g protein; 76g carbohydrates; 17g sugar; 5g fiber; 4mg iron; 203mg calcium.

309 quinoa with mushrooms, kale, and sweet potatoes

PER SERVING: 361 calories; 12g fat (2g saturated fat); 5mg cholesterol; 560mg sodium; 13g protein; 51g carbohydrates; 5g sugar; 6g fiber; 6mg iron; 229mg calcium.

311 skillet-poached huevos rancheros

PER SERVING: 325 calories; 13g fat (6g saturated fat); 232mg cholesterol; 1,119mg sodium; 14g protein; 37g carbohydrates; 7g sugar; 5g fiber; 3mg iron; 115mg calcium.

313 potato, leek, and Feta tart

PER SERVING: 396 calories; 22g fat (9g saturated fat); 27mg cholesterol; 668mg sodium; 7g protein; 44g carbohydrates; 6g sugar; 2g fiber; 2mg iron; 134mg calcium.

317 classic chocolate layer cake
PER SERVING: 1,306 calories; 86g fat (54g saturated fat); 213mg cholesterol; 435mg sodium; 14g protein; 135g carbohydrates; 100g sugar; 4g fiber; 5mg iron; 61mg calcium.

319 raspberry ice
PER SERVING: 193 calories; 6g fat (4g saturated fat); 21mg cholesterol; 7mg sodium; 1g protein; 36g carbohydrates; 29g sugar; 6g fiber; 1mg iron; 31mg calcium.

321 bourbon and orange pecan pie
PER SERVING: 650 calories; 39g fat (13g saturated fat); 125mg cholesterol; 303mg sodium; 7g protein; 74g carbohydrates; 34g sugar; 3g fiber; 2mg iron; 61mg calcium.

323 fried dough with chocolate sauce
PER SERVING: 633 calories; 23g fat (3g saturated fat); 0mg cholesterol; 388mg sodium; 12g protein; 99g carbohydrates; 39g sugar; 2g fiber; 4mg iron; 0mg calcium.

325 peanut butter cup and pretzel terrine
PER SERVING: 340 calories; 19g fat (9g saturated fat); 39mg cholesterol; 213mg sodium; 7g protein; 38g carbohydrates; 30g sugar; 1g fiber; 1mg iron; 135mg calcium.

327 chocolate fudge pie
PER SERVING: 599 calories; 43g fat (26g saturated fat); 180mg cholesterol; 191mg sodium; 7g protein; 51g carbohydrates; 32g sugar; 1g fiber; 2mg iron; 40mg calcium.

328 poached-apricot sundaes with coconut
PER SERVING: 328 calories; 11g fat (7g saturated fat); 25mg cholesterol; 52mg sodium; 3g protein; 56g carbohydrates; 51g sugar; 1g fiber; 0mg iron; 90mg calcium.

328 banana-rum sundaes with toasted pecans
PER SERVING: 397 calories; 25g fat (12g saturated fat); 66mg cholesterol; 48mg sodium; 5g protein; 34g carbohydrates; 25g sugar; 2g fiber; 0mg iron; 110mg calcium.

329 gin-spiked blueberry sundaes
PER SERVING: 188 calories; 9g fat (5g saturated fat); 25mg cholesterol; 35mg sodium; 3g protein; 20g carbohydrates; 18g sugar; 1g fiber; 0mg iron; 82mg calcium.

329 cinnamon-crisp sundaes with chocolate sauce
PER SERVING: 450 calories; 20g fat (11g saturated fat); 48mg cholesterol; 265mg sodium; 7g protein; 62g carbohydrates; 41g sugar; 1g fiber; 2mg iron; 127mg calcium.

331 peanut butter cup cookies
PER COOKIE: 90 calories; 4g fat (2g saturated fat); 10mg cholesterol; 72mg sodium; 1g protein; 12g carbohydrates; 9g sugar; 0g fiber; 0mg iron; 10mg calcium.

333 maple pumpkin pie
PER SERVING: 377 calories; 24g fat (15g saturated fat); 124mg cholesterol; 275mg sodium; 6g protein; 37g carbohydrates; 16g sugar; 3g fiber; 2mg iron; 58mg calcium.

335 berry and ice cream shortcakes
PER SERVING: 397 calories; 18g fat (6g saturated fat); 26mg cholesterol; 572mg sodium; 7g protein; 56g carbohydrates; 26g sugar; 2g fiber; 2mg iron; 113mg calcium.

337 orange–poppy seed shortbread wedges
PER WEDGE: 133 calories; 9g fat (5g saturated fat); 22mg cholesterol; 21mg sodium; 1g protein; 13g carbohydrates; 5g sugar; 0g fiber; 1mg iron; 12mg calcium.

339 chocolate-ricotta icebox cake
PER SERVING: 467 calories; 28g fat (17g saturated fat); 55mg cholesterol; 182mg sodium; 16g protein; 42g carbohydrates; 29g sugar; 1g fiber; 2mg iron; 225mg calcium.

341 easy yellow cupcakes with cream cheese frosting
PER CUPCAKE: 477 calories; 23g fat (14g saturated fat); 96mg cholesterol; 269mg sodium; 5g protein; 64g carbohydrates; 49g sugar; 1g fiber; 1mg iron; 57mg calcium.

341 pb & j cupcake
PER CUPCAKE: 554 calories; 28g fat (15g saturated fat); 96mg cholesterol; 303mg sodium; 8g protein; 70g carbohydrates; 54g sugar; 8g fiber; 1mg iron; 58mg calcium.

341 strawberry hearts cupcake
PER CUPCAKE: 500 calories; 23g fat (14g saturated fat); 96mg cholesterol; 269mg sodium; 5g protein; 69g carbohydrates; 53g sugar; 1g fiber; 1mg iron; 57mg calcium.

341 lemon curd cupcake
PER CUPCAKE: 523 calories; 23g fat (14g saturated fat); 102mg cholesterol; 275mg sodium; 5g protein; 74g carbohydrates; 58g sugar; 1g fiber; 1mg iron; 57mg calcium.

341 triple chocolate cupcake
PER CUPCAKE: 599 calories; 30g fat (18g saturated fat); 102mg cholesterol; 324mg sodium; 7g protein; 80g carbohydrates; 59g sugar; 1g fiber; 2mg iron; 78mg calcium.

343 caramel-almond ice cream torte
PER SERVING: 290 calories; 14g fat (7g saturated fat); 33mg cholesterol; 120mg sodium; 6g protein; 38g carbohydrates; 32g sugar; 1g fiber; 0mg iron; 117mg calcium.

C

REAL SIMPLE

managing editor Kristin van Ogtrop
creative director Janet Froelich
executive editor Sarah Humphreys
deputy managing editor Jacklyn Monk
managing editor, RealSimple.com
Kathleen Murray Harris

STAFF FOR THIS BOOK

food director Allie Lewis Clapp
art director Eva Spring
senior editor Lygeia Grace
food assistant Lindsay Funston
contributing editor Candy Gianetti
photo director Casey Tierney
deputy photo editor
Lauren Reichbach Epstein
photo archivist Brian Madigan
copy chief Nancy Negovetich
copy editors Benjamin Ake, Jenny Brown,
Pamela Grossman
research chief Westry Green
researcher Kaitlyn Pirie
art assistant Jennica Johnstone
production director Jeff Nesmith
production manager Joan Weinstein
imaging director Richard Prue
imaging manager Claudio Muller

publisher Kevin White
associate publisher Melissa Gasper
senior vice president, consumer marketing
Carrie Goldin
vice president, marketing Sarah Kate Ellis

TIME HOME ENTERTAINMENT

publisher Richard Fraiman
general manager Steven Sandonato
executive director, marketing services
Carol Pittard
director, retail & special sales Tom Mifsud
director, new product development
Peter Harper
director, bookazine development
& marketing Laura Adam
publishing director, brand marketing
Joy Butts
assistant general counsel Helen Wan

marketing manager Victoria Alfonso
design & prepress manager
Anne-Michelle Gallero
book production manager
Susan Chodakiewicz

SPECIAL THANKS

recipe developers Kristen Evans,
Cyd McDowell, Kate Merker, Sara
Quessenberry, Jenny Rosenstrach
recipe testers Kristen Evans, Vanessa
Seder, Susan Streight, Amy Vuoso,
Caroline Wright, Chelsea Zimmer
food stylists Victoria Granof, Jee Levin,
Cyd McDowell, Carrie Purcell,
Sara Quessenberry, Maggie Ruggiero,
Susan Spungen, Susan Sugarman,
Susie Theodorou
prop stylists Angharad Bailey, Jocelyne
Beaudoin, Heather Chontos, Helen
Crowther, Cindy DiPrima, Michele Faro,
Lynsey Fryers, Terry Mainord, PJ Mehaffey,
Jeffrey W. Miller, Pam Morris, Leslie
Siegel, Loren Simons, Theo Vamvounakis,
Deborah Williams, David Yarritu
thanks also to Christine Austin, Jeremy
Biloon, Glenn Buonocore, Jim Childs,
Rose Cirrincione, Jacqueline Fitzgerald,
Carrie Frazier, Lauren Hall, Kelly
Holechek, Suzanne Janso, Malena Jones,
Brynn Joyce, Mona Li, Robert Marasco,
Kimberly Marshall, Amy Migliaccio,
Brooke Reger, Dave Rozzelle, Ilene
Schreider, Adriana Tierno, Vanessa Wu

PHOTO CREDITS

COVER: Christopher Baker, photographer;
Jeffrey W. Miller, prop stylist; Maggie
Ruggiero, food stylist
Quentin Bacon: *pages 134, 138, 154, 166,
178, 208, 226, 238, 260, 288, 304 (right), 310*
Christopher Baker: *pages 10 (left, right),
12 (right), 13 (right), 17 (left), 78, 144, 174,
236, 242, 282, 294, 302, 306, 308, 312,
318, 329 (left)*
Hans Gissinger: *pages 34, 40, 42, 94, 128, 184*
Ditte Isager: *page 11 (left)*
John Kernick: *page 330*

Yunhee Kim: *pages 180, 305 (left)*
Charles Masters: *pages 14 (right), 68, 122,
136, 150, 156, 340*
Ellie Miller: *pages 50, 60, 82, 86, 98, 102,
106, 110, 114, 118*
Marcus Nilsson: *pages 52, 66, 76, 108,
186, 194, 196, 198, 202, 204, 206, 220, 240,
268, 270*
José Picayo: *pages 16 (right), 28, 88, 100,
130, 164, 168, 176, 182, 192, 200, 218, 232,
252, 266, 278, 336*
Con Poulos: *pages 8, 12 (left), 14 (left),
15 (left), 16 (left), 18, 22, 26, 54, 58 (left,
right), 59 (left, right), 70, 84, 142, 148, 172,
216, 254, 284, 286, 290, 296, 316*
David Prince: *pages 11 (right), 13 (left),
15 (right), 24, 38, 48, 56, 64, 72, 92, 116,
132, 140, 152, 158, 162, 188, 190, 224, 230,
244, 248, 258, 272, 274 (left, right), 275 (left,
right), 276, 280, 304 (left), 305 (right), 320,
322, 324, 326, 328 (left, right), 329 (right),
332, 334, 342*
Jonny Valiant: *pages 32, 104, 160, 212, 300*
Anna Williams: *page 90*
James Wojcik: *page 17 (right)*
Romulo Yanes: *pages 30, 36, 46, 62, 80, 96,
112, 124, 126, 146, 210, 222, 228, 234, 246,
250, 256, 264, 298*

Copyright © 2011
Time Home Entertainment Inc.
Published by Real Simple Books, an imprint of
Time Home Entertainment Inc.
135 West 50th Street
New York, NY 10020

First printing 2011
ISBN 10: 1-60320-875-5
ISBN 13: 978-1-60320-875-8

Printed in the USA

We welcome your comments and suggestions
about Real Simple Books. Please e-mail us at
books@realsimple.com. To order any of our
Collector's Edition books, please call us at
1-800-327-6388 (Monday through Friday, 7 A.M.
to 8 P.M. CST, or Saturday, 7 A.M. to 6 P.M. CST).